The Love of China

The Love of China

Anthony Lawrence

OCTOPUS

Contents

page 1 The 4,000-year-old 'Greeting the Guests' pine-tree on one of the 72 peaks of the Huangshan range in Anhui province.
page 2/3 Against a back-drop of strangely shaped limestone hills, houseboats drift down the Li River near the southern city of Guilin.

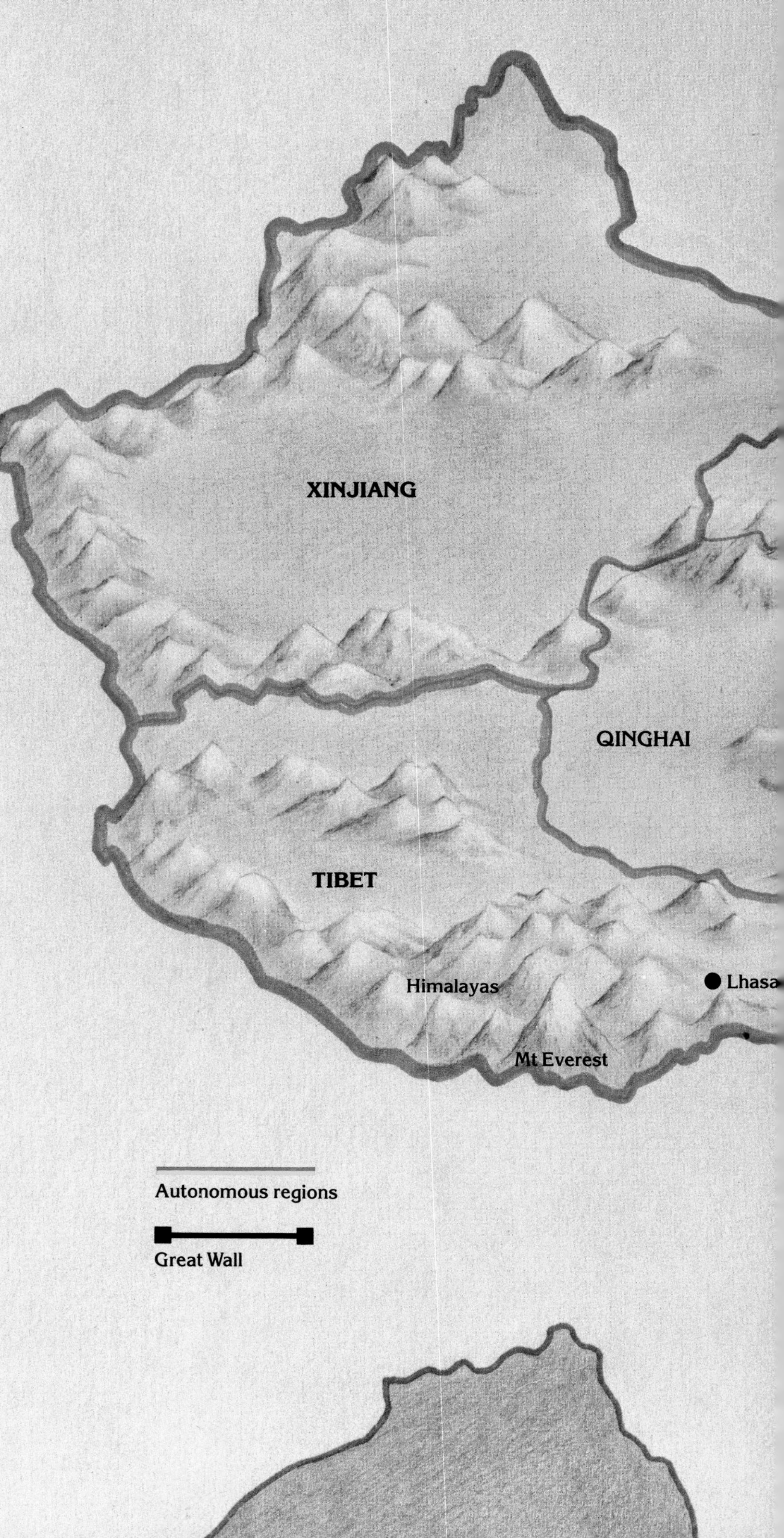

First published in 1979 by
Octopus Books Limited 59 Grosvenor Street London W1

ISBN 0 7064 1140 4
Produced by Mandarin Publishers Limited
22a Westlands Road Quarry Bay Hong Kong
Printed in Italy - Nuova Grafica Moderna S.p.A. - Verona

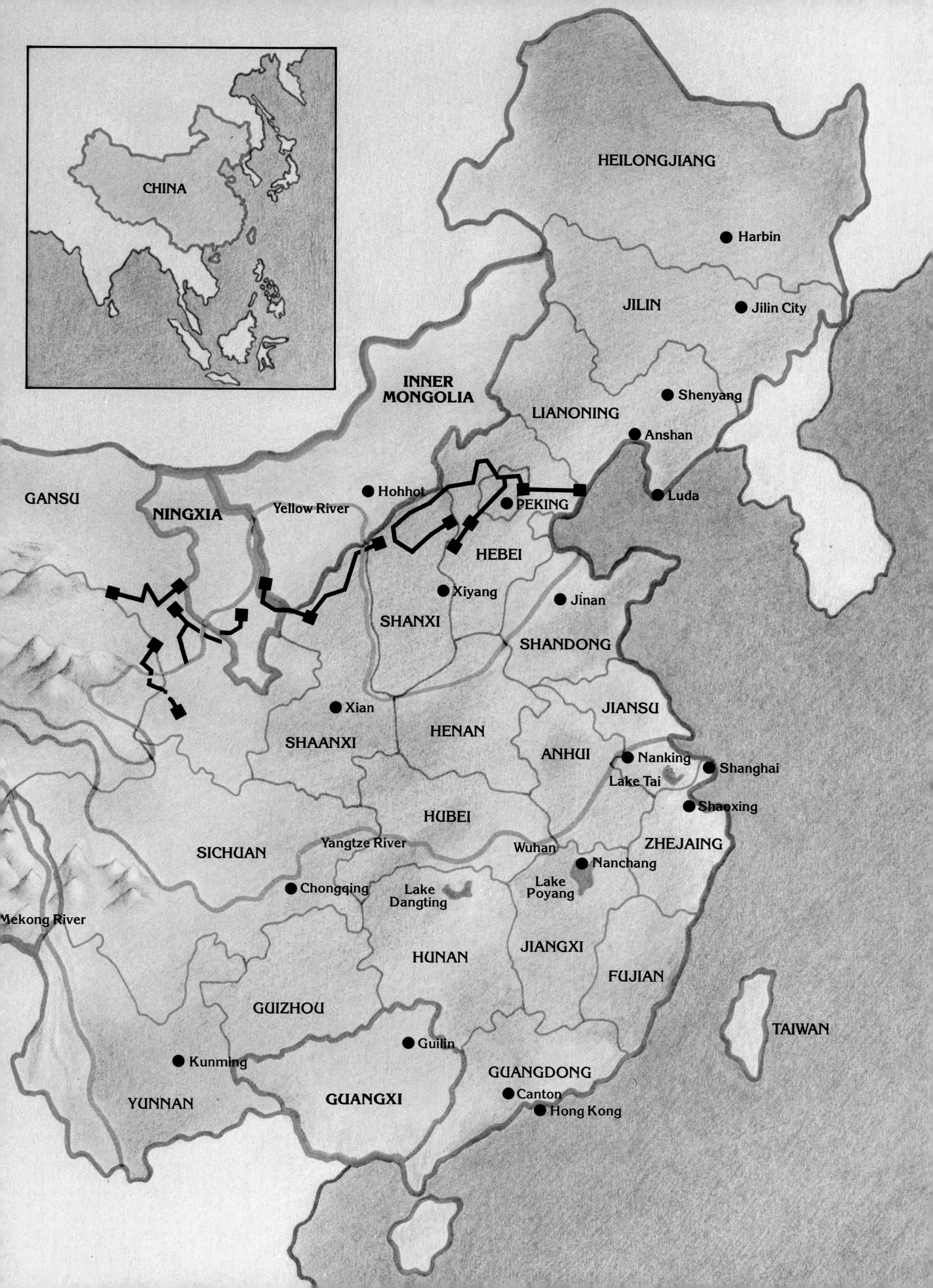
CHINA
HEILONGJIANG
Harbin
JILIN
Jilin City
INNER MONGOLIA
LIANONING
Shenyang
Anshan
Luda
GANSU
NINGXIA
Hohhot
Yellow River
PEKING
HEBEI
Xiyang
Jinan
SHANXI
SHANDONG
Xian
JIANSU
HENAN
SHAANXI
ANHUI
Nanking
Shanghai
Lake Tai
Shaoxing
HUBEI
Yangtze River
SICHUAN
Wuhan
ZHEJAING
Nanchang
Lake Poyang
Chongqing
Lake Dangting
Mekong River
JIANGXI
HUNAN
FUJIAN
GUIZHOU
TAIWAN
Guilin
Kunming
GUANGDONG
Canton
Hong Kong
YUNNAN
GUANGXI

Introduction

(*Right*) The giant panda has proved a popular unofficial ambassador for China in western zoos. Found in remote areas of Gansu and Sichuan provinces the pandas were at one time almost extinct, but now they are a protected species and both hunting them and destruction of their habitat by unplanned tree-felling are forbidden. The Chinese will tell you that pandas are no longer afraid of man and sometimes they even visit lumber camps during the evening to warm themselves at the cookhouse fire.

China is a country of enormous size and variety of climate and landscape. The Chinese people number nearly one thousand million. Though they almost all have black hair and smooth eyelids, there is as much difference in build and temperament between those of the northern provinces and those of the south as there is in Europe between Scandinavians and Latins.

Variety is the keynote of the country. In the northeast province of Heilongjiang (Black Dragon River) the Chinese inhabit great forests and plains where in winter the temperature plummets to −40°C. Two thousand miles further south, on Hainan Island, they grow pineapples and rubber and sweat in the tropical heat. In the east are ancient cities, flourishing farming communes and growing industrial centres, in the west high mountains, deserts and grasslands. Each of the 26 provinces has its own dialects, customs and traditions. But all the people in these widely differing areas are Chinese, and they all know themselves to be citizens of the land they call Zhong Guo (Chung Kuo) – the Central Kingdom.

For many centuries the Chinese felt that their country was indeed the central kingdom of the world, that it represented human civilization and that outside the imperial frontiers were only barbarians and minority groups. And, during the long period when Europe was going through the Dark Ages, the advanced state of Chinese culture, science, politics, literature and arts justified their view.

Chinese civilization is not the oldest in the world, but it is the most continuous. The thousands of written characters or ideograms that the Chinese use singly or in pairs to represent words have changed little over the last 2,000 years, and this written language has been a great unifying force. Writing is the same for everyone, however much local languages and dialects may hinder spoken contacts between people from different regions. Now the teaching of a common speech (Putong Hua) based on Mandarin is official policy.

All Chinese are conscious of their long past stretching back into the mists of legend. Mythical kings are supposed to have invented clothing, cooking, marriage and methods of government.

Excavations near today's capital, Peking, have brought to light the bones of Peking Man, a forerunner of modern man who lived in caves 500,000 years ago. Small kingdoms emerged about 4,000 years ago along the Yellow River, in north China, where local rulers fought and intrigued for survival or domination. The office of emperor seems to have existed from very early times, but often the power of the emperor was very limited; he was the go-between, praying to heaven on behalf of the people for abundant harvests.

Chinese civilization was well advanced 1,500 years before Christ. Under the Shang dynasty cities grew, canals and roads were built, craftsmen fashioned masterly bronze sacrificial vessels, codes of law were established, and 'scholars' – men learned in religious and human affairs – were valued as advisers and tutors by China's great families.

The most famous scholar-philosopher, Confucius, was born in 551 BC, in what is now the northern province of Shandong (Shantung). He taught the obedience of sons to the father, of subjects to the emperor, of the emperor to heaven. For over 2,000 years his teachings formed the moral code of Chinese intellectuals and officials.

The first unification of all China's states came in the 3rd century BC under the rule of Shih Huang Ti. A man of humble origins, he wrought such great changes and developments in Chinese life that his own small state of Ch'in gave its name to the whole country, which the world has called China ever since. He com-

新中国兒童海军

(*Left*) The bronze horse rests his foot on a flying swallow to show how fast he gallops. This was one of the bronzes unearthed in a tomb dating back to the eastern Han dynasty (25-220AD) at Wuwei in northern China not far from the Great Wall. The horse was part of an exhibition shown in the West in recent years, but now the Chinese authorities have decided it is too precious a work of art to leave China again.

(*Far left*) The Chinese characters round the small boy's cap read 'New China Children's Navy'. He is one of millions of boys and girls who live in the towns and cities of China belonging to children's organizations. They are taught games, drill and patriotism. Chinese children are very friendly and always leave a lasting impression on foreign visitors. Most tours of China include a visit to a 'Children's Palace' where selected children go for games and training.

pletely reorganized the administration and standardized Chinese script, weights, measures and even the gauge of wagon tracks. But he was a tyrant who ran a dictatorial military state in which scholars were buried alive and books were burned. As soon as he died, six rebellions broke out.

In the next 2,000 years China was to see the rise and fall of many other famous dynasties – the Han, the T'ang, the Sung and the Ming. Under these the arts and literature flourished in the cities and imperial courts. China was also invaded by Mongols, in the 13th century, and Manchus, in the 17th. After their conquests, these invaders were so impressed by the culture and customs of the Chinese that they adopted them themselves.

In the last century China was exposed to the West. European and American merchants demanded trade with the country and brought with them new technology, illegal opium and modern weapons of war. The 20th century has been crowded with drama. It has seen the end of imperial rule, the setting up of a republic, invasion by Japan, civil war and, in 1949, the take-over by the communists under Mao Tse-tung.

Under its communist leaders China is now engaged in a programme of modernizing agriculture, industry, defence, science and technology, to raise the country to the level of current world powers by the end of the century. The Chinese know they have the required skills, energy, intelligence and discipline. But the obstacles are enormous. The country is the third largest in the world (after the Soviet Union and Canada) but of its vast 3¾ million square miles, only about 14 per cent is cultivable. The rest is mountain, water and desert. In recent decades the Chinese have greatly increased their harvests with fertilizers, irrigation and the terracing of mountain slopes. In the more fertile areas – especially the great rice communes of the south and the wheatfields of the northern plains – the ripening grain stretching to the horizon gives an unforgettable impression of prosperous self-sufficiency. But keeping the people fed is still a problem. Although family planning is widely practised – especially in the towns where propaganda and control are more effective – the population increases by about 12 million a year. So agriculture remains a priority – and more than 80 per cent of the population works on the land.

However, there is also continuous pressure to industrialize. New factories rear up beside the sites of ancient cities, more steelworks are built, more oil-fields open. This is the drama of the Chinese contemporary scene – the battle for material progress while the life of the fields, the rhythm of planting and harvest, continues as it has for thousands of years. It is this, as well as meeting its cheerful, friendly people, that makes a journey to China an experience no traveller can forget.

Manchuria

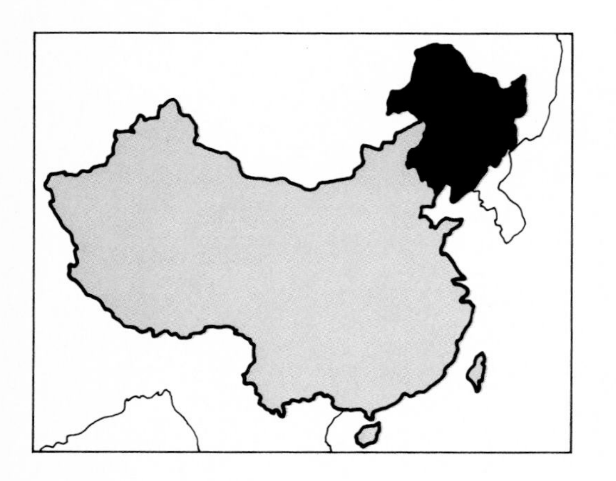

The North-East is the industrial heartland of the Chinese People's Republic. It used to be called Manchuria, for it was once the home of the Manchus, a fierce and powerful people who in the mid-17th century conquered all China. They ruled as the Ch'ing Dynasty until 1911, when China became a republic.

The last years of the Manchu rulers were a time of weakness and decadence, and foreign powers exploited the situation. The Russians and the Japanese set up competing zones of influence in Manchuria, clashed in the Russo-Japanese war, and dominated the area for the first decades of the 20th century.

Now both the Russians and the Japanese have gone, and the Manchus have long since been reduced to the status of one of China's 50 minority groups. Where their cavalry rode the great northern plains, men of the Chinese People's Liberation Army open up farmland and guard the frontiers.

Former Manchuria is now three provinces – *Heilongjiang, Jilin (Kirin), and Liaoning*. The most northerly region of China, it is a wild, hard country with forest-covered mountains in the north and southeast and a huge windswept plain in the centre. In Heilongjiang, which has 2,500 miles of frontier with the Soviet Union, the winters are long and almost unbearably cold, with razor-like winds blowing in from Siberia and the Mongolian Plateau. Because of its industries (it is known as 'the cradle of electricity') and national communications links, the province is of vital importance, and more and more workers are being moved there.

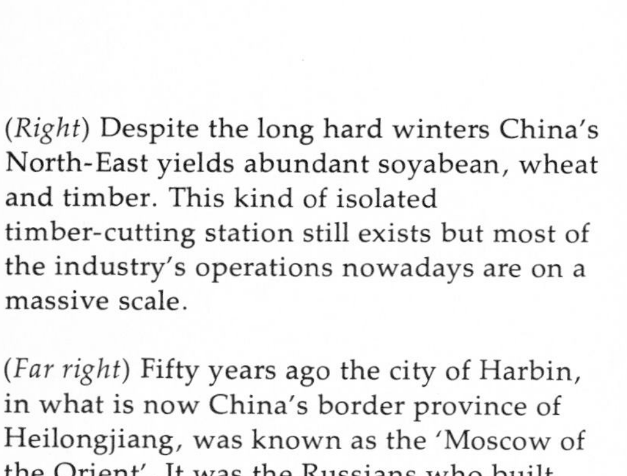

(*Right*) Despite the long hard winters China's North-East yields abundant soyabean, wheat and timber. This kind of isolated timber-cutting station still exists but most of the industry's operations nowadays are on a massive scale.

(*Far right*) Fifty years ago the city of Harbin, in what is now China's border province of Heilongjiang, was known as the 'Moscow of the Orient'. It was the Russians who built the Trans-Siberian Railway across the province to Vladivostock and turned Harbin from a village into the centre of a communications network. Many Russian-style buildings survived after Soviet armies and technicians had left, including the picturesque old Cathedral of St. Nicholas, attended by a dwindling band of White Russians who settled in China's North-East after the Russian Revolution. Now they have resettled elsewhere or died and the church has gone, too. A public park covers its site.

(*Below*) Changchun is famous for its enormous car and truck plant, but to the south of the city lies the great South Lake surrounded by parks. The Chinese, whether scholars or car-assemblers, find special pleasure in lakes, bridges of irregular design and small pavilions.

(*Insets*) Before the Manuchus swept down from the north to conquer China in 1644, their imperial capital in Manchuria was the city of Shenyang, and in the middle of that city stands the majestic imperial palace. The tombs of two great Manchu emperors and their wives shown here are a dozen miles to the north of the city, at Beiling. The Manchus, although they were a northern, alien race, admired and imitated Chinese culture and civilization, including the architectural style of their tombs and palaces. Official titles on buildings were in Chinese characters as well as in Manchu.

(*Above*) A street in Shenyang City. The monotonous line of buildings recalls the official architectural style of Occupation Japanese, when Japanese forces held Manchuria and Japanese big business and industry were developing rapidly in all of this north-eastern region of China. Trees bursting into spring leaf help alleviate the drabness. Sustained programmes of tree planting have done much to improve the appearance of many of China's modern cities which are planned for utility rather than aesthetics. In Shenyang trees also provide welcome shade in the short hot summer.

Harbin, the capital of Heilongjiang, is a flourishing city of 2 million people. It was founded 80 years ago as a junction station on a branch of the Russian Trans-Siberian Railway that cut across Manchuria. In the early 1930s half Harbin's inhabitants were Russians, and even today the city's general plan shows Russian influence, as do many of its buildings and monuments. The principal theatre, which looks like a provincial version of Moscow's Bolshoi Theatre, and the Workers' University, the tallest building, are both Russian-built.

In the early years of the 20th century the Japanese extended their influence into Manchuria. In those days of China's weakness, Japan intrigued with Chinese warlords and generals. In 1933 Japan occupied Manchuria. Japanese trading firms followed the Japanese bayonets and Japanese technology developed the region.

In the last 30 years the Chinese authorities have greatly developed the industries of the North-East (which account for at least a third of all the country's heavy industry) and have invited many foreign visitors to see the region. Many of them, knowing nothing of the region's history, have attributed all its astonishing industrial development to China's communist revolution, not realizing that it started long before.

Harbin has electrical engineering plants and boiler and turbine factories, and about 100 miles northwest of the city lies China's most publicized oil-field, Daqing (Taching), which sprawls over a huge area. Daqing is held up as a model industrial undertaking. The first well was sunk in a frozen field in 1960, and now half a million people live in the vicinity, working the continuously expanding oil-field, tilling the surrounding land and maintaining a large town, so that Daqing is self-supporting as well as supplying China with much of its oil.

The industries of Jilin province include the great motor-car and truck plant at Changchun, the petrochemical plants and paper mills of Jilin City, and the huge steelworks of Anshan. Shenyang (Mukden), capital of Liaoning province, has been called 'the Pittsburgh of China'.

The great plain on which the industries of the three provinces have developed is also devoted to farming. Once it was known as the northern wilderness, but the many state farms of modern times have greatly changed the

(*Above*) Shenyang's two and a half million people – four million if you include the suburbs – serve scores of large-scale factories and refineries and hundreds of smaller plants. Shenyang is a rail centre in China's North-East which links it with Fushun, the coal-mining centre, and the steel city of Anshan. This area is the main industrial base not only of the North-East but of China as a whole, and it is expanding all the time.

scene. The plain is one of the world's greatest producers of soya beans – for the Chinese a protein substitute for milk and cheese. From the beans they make a nutritionally-rich, milky white drink and a soft creamy food called *dou fu*. The most southerly of the three provinces – Liaoning – produces most of China's apple crop.

Where the soil is not rich enough for farming, great pasturelands support sheep stations and cattle-farms, from which sheepskins, hides and meat are shipped to the cities.

The mountain forests of pine and fir supply at least a quarter of China's timber needs. The forests of the Changbai (Ch'angpai) mountains in Jilin province also supply the root *ginseng*, which the Chinese believe to be nature's most effective medicine for invigorating the aged or enfeebled.

Despite all the modernization and industrial development of the North-East, the relics of its past, the traces of the great days of the Manchus, are still preserved. In Shenyang stands a large imperial palace built entirely of wood. Majestic and graceful, it incorporates 70 buildings in which are preserved ceramics, pottery, paintings, jewellery and antique books. North of Shenyang is the impressive mausoleum of the Manchu emperor Tai Zong (Tai Tsung), which is sometimes compared to the famous tombs of the Ming emperors near Peking. And to the south, there survive in the beautiful Chienshan Mountains, many Buddhist monasteries and Taoist temples built between the 9th and 18th centuries.

At the most southerly point of the North-East region is the Port Arthur-Dairen district. It is known as Lüda in Chinese, made up of the first parts of the Chinese names for Port Arthur (Lüshun) and Dairen (Dalian). After the departure of the Japanese at the end of World War Two, this area was set up as a joint Soviet-Chinese naval base until 1955, when Soviet troops were withdrawn by agreement. The port of Dairen can accommodate vessels of up to 20,000 tons along three miles of piers. And Port Arthur, surrounded by a ring of protective mountains and ice-free in winter, has a wide, deep harbour that provides shelter for several dozen warships.

Inner Mongolia and The Far West

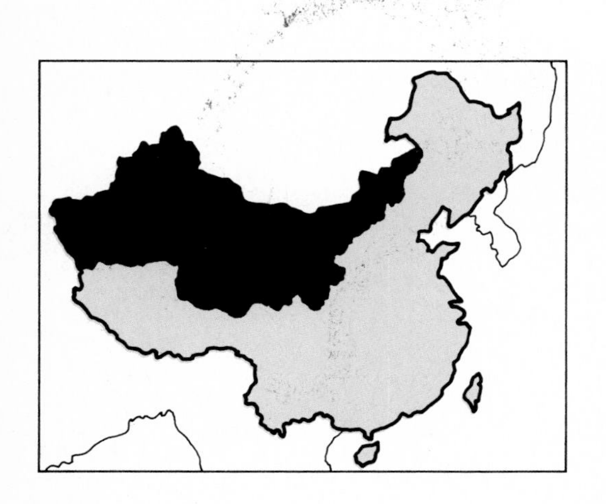

Inner Mongolia is a huge province stretching for more than 1,000 miles across the north of China; but relatively few people live there, because most of it is desert. From this area in ancient days, powerful nomad tribes constantly threatened the security of China, raiding the northern plains in search of loot and of grazing land for their horses and cattle.

To stop their incursions the Chinese built the Great Wall. The rulers of China's early states were already in the habit of constructing defence walls round their small domains, and when the Emperor Chin Shih Huang Ti unified the country, he incorporated some of these existing walls into his own new Great Wall. Later emperors strengthened and extended the Wall. At one stage they even built a second wall because they so feared barbarian attacks. But for much of the time China was so powerful and controlled so many of the northern lands that the Wall was superfluous.

Songs and folk-ballads still tell the story of how the Wall was built, of the forced labour, of the southerners who succumbed to the harsh weather of the north and whose bones were shovelled in with the Wall's foundations, and of the young wife who – through many verses of one song – looks for her husband among the construction gangs and tearfully finds his body at last when part of the Wall suffers temporary collapse.

The extensions to the current Wall down the centuries made it a vast monument known throughout most of the world. It was the only man-made construction that American astronauts could identify from their earth-circling spaceship. Much of it now lies in ruins; but thousands can visit a restored section of it near Peking.

How effective was the Wall in protecting China from the barbarians? Like all such barriers it served little purpose unless it was resolutely manned, and when Chinese dynasties were corrupt and their soldiers had lost heart, the Wall could not stop an invasion.

It failed to stop the Mongols. And this is perhaps not surprising in view of the fact that by the mid-13th century this powerful nation of warring nomads led by Genghis Khan had conquered nearly all of the known world. The Mongols swept down into the Chinese plains like an onrushing sea, and within a few years they had occupied the entire country. The inheritor of Genghis Khan's empire, his grandson Kublai Khan, established himself in Peking and in about 1280 built there a magnificent new capital which he called Khan-Balik.

Merchants and craftsmen of Asia and Europe were soon visiting the grand new city; and among them was the Venetian, Marco Polo, who lived in China for about 20 years, took an official post under the Mongol emperor and wrote the famous account of his travels to and through China.

The Mongols in China soon lost their taste for war. They succumbed to the ease and pleasure of Chinese life, and within a few decades they began to lose control of the country until their power scarcely extended beyond Peking and a few garrison towns. One uprising followed another as China grew steadily poorer under its feeble administration. Finally, in 1368, the Mongol rulers and their followers were thrown from power, many were massacred and the survivors retreated north beyond the Great Wall to the lands of their origin. That is where their descendants live today, in a vast area of desert and steppe.

The most northerly, or outer, half of this area is the Mongolian People's Republic, an independent nation which is an ally of the Soviet Union. The southern, or inner, half of the area is Inner Mongolia (or, to give it its full name, the Inner Mongolian Autonomous Region), a province of China. Like other

(*Right*) Hard climates produce tough wrestlers and riders – Mongol herdsmen of northern China follow a long tradition of fierce competition in outdoor sports. There are more Mongols in China than in the neighbouring Mongolian People's Republic and, as a minority group, they are concerned with preserving their identity. The story of their great war leader Genghis Khan remains very much alive with them. The Chinese authorities have pursued various policies aimed at consolidating their loyalty to the People's Republic and they have also moved millions of racial Chinese up into Inner Mongolia where they now greatly outnumber the Mongols.

(*Above right*) The commune system has long been applied to Inner Mongolia and there has been a steady movement in recent years away from scattered nomad communities to the settled village. But most Mongols are still engaged in breeding sheep and horses and until recently it is the Chinese, the Hans, who have been mainly concerned with farming and industrial development.

(*Below right*) Horse-riding is still the passion of the Mongols, the Uighurs, the Kazakhs and all the peoples of the great plains of the North and West. They learn to ride bareback and gallop at breakneck speed to round up the herds.

(*Below*) As in communes everywhere in China, training in the militia is part of life for all able-bodied men and women.

so-called autonomous regions, it is governed from Peking – although the local people choose their own party committees and provincial council.

Nowadays the Mongols, at least in the cities, are outnumbered ten to one by Chinese who have been moved into the province. Yet something of the old Mongol toughness remains. Most of Inner Mongolia is a huge, largely barren plateau where grass grows only during the short summers and where many Mongols are still horsemen, herding and tending sheep, cattle and horses as they have done for centuries.

The French Catholic missionary Father Huc, who travelled more than 100 years ago through the land which is now Inner Mongolia, said that the people there were so used to riding (on camels as well as horses) that as soon as they set foot on the ground they felt unsure of themselves and walked in a clumsy fashion. 'And if they travel at night,' he wrote, 'they often sleep in the saddle to save themselves the trouble of getting off and resting on the ground. You sometimes have the strange spectacle of a caravan halted at some good pasturage for the beasts to eat, while each rider, supported between the humps of his camel, is plunged in deepest sleep.'

Mutton is a popular food among the Mongols. The tails of fat sheep are a special delicacy. And throughout China a well-known meal is the so-called Mongolian hot-pot, at which the diners sit round a circular vessel filled with boiling water heated by a small charcoal burner and dip pieces of mutton and vegetable in the water until they are cooked. These meals resemble nomadic camp-fires on the northern plains.

Father Huc wrote that the winters in Inner Mongolia are so cold that the mercury in a thermometer freezes. He described how the herdsmen's beasts are trapped in huge drifts of wind-driven snow, into which the herdsmen plunge with wild shouts to retrieve their animals and take them to shelter.

Even today many of the Mongols still live in *yurts*, their traditional circular tents of felt. And horsemanship is still highly esteemed. Whenever the official Inner Mongolian equestrian team stages a show on the 2,000-metre-long racecourse at the foot of the Daqing (Taching) Mountains outside Huhehot, the capital of the province, vast crowds gather to watch and criticize. The horseback gymnastics draw most applause. Six-man pyramids bestride three fast-moving

North of Peking beyond the valleys and hillsides of the Ming Tombs the Great Wall of China snakes across the mountains – the barrier planned 2,000 years ago to keep the barbarian world from disturbing the serenity of the Central Kingdom. At first it was built of mud but in the Ming Dynasty (1368–1644) its surface was covered with bricks and stone. It is about 20 feet high with battlements facing the north, barbarian, side and its total length is given as about 4,000 miles. It is said to be haunted by the ghosts of untold thousands of forced labourers who worked and died there.

horses, and men and women riding at a fast gallop flip rattan wreaths off high posts with flashing swords or shoot at moving targets.

But this life is changing under the pressure of large-scale campaigns to reclaim the desert and increase food supplies. For this purpose, great stretches of netting are laid across some areas of shifting sand to reduce its movement, and then tough grass is sown to bind the sand. Industrial development is also being stepped up in the area.

The Mongols have lost much of their grazing ground to the state farms, and sometimes they have resisted this. So this area of tensions between the indigenous peoples and the state administrators is not one to which foreigners are usually taken. They are more likely to visit the fertile and prosperous lands in southwest Inner Mongolia, where the Yellow River flows in a broad stream beyond the Great Wall. Here irrigation channels criss-cross the fields, iron and steel are produced, and other industries are being expanded and diversified. Railways link the area with all the main regions of China.

Stretching westwards from Inner Mongolia to the very centre of the Asian landmass is China's Far West – the provinces of Xinjiang (Sinkiang), Qinghai and Gansu (Kansu). You can fly there now, or take the jeep road, but in former times it was a journey to daunt all but the bravest. The bones of soldiers, merchants and camels whitened along the windswept desert trails. An ancient poet wrote: 'A vast expanse of sand with no sign of human life; only white grass grows amid ten thousand rocks.' Another complained of the barbarism of the area. 'The warm winds of spring,' he wrote, referring to the joys of culture, 'never cross the Yumen pass.'

This unwelcoming desert area, approached from Peking through the narrow neck of the Gansu Corridor, has always been at once the link and the no-man's-land between empires and cultures and has played a major part in China's history. For through the Far West wound the famous Silk Road, the trade route by which the products of China were exchanged for those of the Middle East and Europe.

And by the southern leg of this route Buddhism was brought to China from India, as evidenced by the many famous Buddhist cave sanctuaries along the road, containing statues, wall-paintings and inscriptions.

(*Left*) Through sandy wastes and rock-strewn desert the caravans of former ages journeyed out through China's far west provinces to trade with the West. These are the least populated areas of all China – less than four inhabitants to the square mile.

(*Far left above*) Like other nomad people the Kazakhs have always in the past lived in tents, known in the local language as 'yurts'. They vary in style according to the minority group but are usually made of thick felt which resists the wind and sometimes are well furnished inside with carpets.

(*Far left below*) The western province of Xinjiang has minority groups like the Uighurs and the Kazakhs – horsemen and cattle breeders whose grazing lands formerly stretched both sides of today's Sino-Soviet frontier. The Kazakhs of Xinjiang share a common history, as well as a common Turkic language, with the Russian Kazakhs. They are Muslims but not very strict in following Islamic practices. To consolidate security millions of Chinese from further east have been sent to Xinjiang in the past two decades and they now outnumber the minority groups there.

The Silk Road was opened up in the first century AD. In return for China's much-prized silk, Rome provided glassware (which the Chinese did not yet know how to make), metal ware and woollen tapestries. The route began near the present-day Xian (Sian) and led through Xinjiang province south of the Tien Shan mountains as far as Kashgar, through bitter cold and snow over the high Pamir range, down through Persia and finally to Antioch, the capital of Syria – a total distance of about 4,000 miles.

Today most of the Far West is comprised by the vast province of Xinjiang (known officially as the Xinjiang Uygur Autonomous Region), which occupies 625,000 square miles – about a sixth of China. Xinjiang means 'New Frontier' and Uygur is the name given to a large Muslim minority group in the region. There are 12 other minority groups, including the Kazakhs, Huis, Tartars, Mongols and Manchus. These are the remnants of once-powerful nations that threatened or actually invaded China in days gone by. Now many of them are herdsmen, rearing horses and tending sheep, wearing national costume and preserving their traditional dances – hardy inhabitants of the great infertile wastes.

The minority groups are outnumbered in Xinjiang by Chinese, many of whom arrived as soldiers in the construction units of the People's Liberation Army. Xinjiang adjoins the Soviet Union and is a sensitive area, for it contains the testing grounds for long-range nuclear rockets. But in China the army has additional tasks besides training and fighting. In Xinjiang it has built roads, improved irrigation and laid out and developed state farms. And when the troops have completed their military service, they often stay on as settlers.

Apart from the soldiers, many ordinary citizens from such eastern cities as Shanghai have volunteered, or have been drafted, to go to Xinjiang and work for its development. The volunteers have included many young people. The results have been impressive. More state farms have been established, the large scale ones almost entirely mechanized; more desert has been converted to grassland; harvests have been greatly increased in the arable areas; more schools, hospitals and factories have been built, and new oil-fields are being opened.

The Yellow River

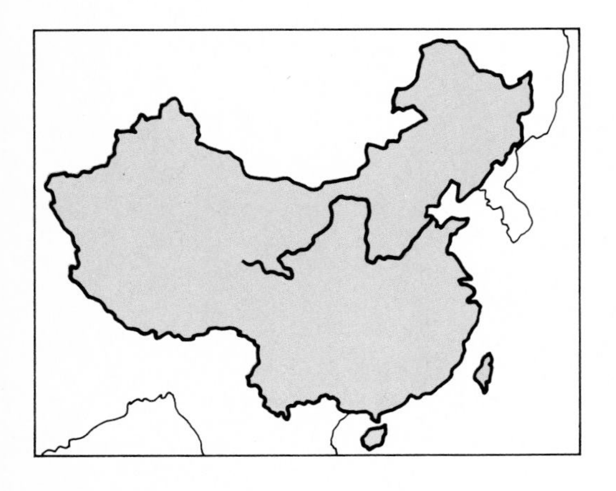

The Yellow River is the home of China's earliest civilization; along its valleys and those of its tributaries successive emperors established their cities and palaces. Such places as Zhengzhou (Chengchow), Luoyang and Chang An became famous in China's history. But the river is also known as China's Sorrow, because of the millions of lives lost in its countless floods or from famine when it dried up and the crops failed.

The Yellow River, China's second longest waterway, rises in the Bayan Kara Mountains in the remote western province of Qinghai (Chinghai) and flows through seven provinces on its way to the sea in the northeast. At the beginning of its course it thunders with the speed of an express train through deep gorges, losing altitude rapidly and providing energy for the power plants serving the northwest of China. It passes the great industrial city of Lanzhou (Lanchow), with its petrochemical complexes, heavy engineering works and steel mills stretching for 50 kilometres along the river bank, then meanders far to the north, through fertile farming country still irrigated by canals built 2,000 years ago. Here no one would believe that this placid stream flowing steadily through lush fields and plantations could ever be called China's Sorrow. But 200 miles further on the river swings south again, and now it moves through a strange area known as the loess-lands – more than half a million square kilometres of fine, yellow or light-chocolate coloured, dusty soil, lying thick on the hills and upland plateaux.

Loess is a strange soil – so fine that when it is rubbed between the fingers it disappears into the pores of the skin, yet so firm at the same time *en masse* that when excavations are dug in it, perpendicular walls more than 100 feet high will hold steady without collapsing. In fact, in many of the villages people live in caves hollowed out of the loess. It was in loess caves in and around Yenan that communist forces weary from the famous Long March found a refuge from Chiang Kai-shek's armies.

Nobody knows just how this expanse of loess developed. One theory is that it was carried by the wind from the far north. Others think it was there as mud when all North China lay under the sea millions of years ago. Whatever its origins, it has always been a problem for the Chinese. When the rains come it is washed away in thousands of tons and carried by countless streams and tributaries into the Yellow River.

From then on the river really is yellow as it meanders east and then northeast across the North China plains. And on this slow stage of its journey it continuously deposits the silt it contains, so that its bed keeps rising. To prevent the river overflowing, scores of thousands of peasants are mobilized every year to strengthen and raise the banks. As a result, in some places the river seems to be a high causeway. The river has occasionally changed course unexpectedly. In the middle of the last century, for example, it switched direction about 45 degrees to the north through Shandong province, causing great loss of life and damage to thousands of villages.

On many occasions in China's history famine faced the peasants of the northern plains when the rains failed in the Yellow River's upper reaches and the great stream shrank to a trickle. For several weeks in 1960 the Yellow River dried up completely in Honan and Shantung provinces, and the 57 million people of Shantung province lost their entire harvest. That was the time of the Three Bad Years in China, when many went hungry.

It is not surprising, then, that the aim of every Chinese dynasty down through the ages has been to tame the Yellow River. In ancient times the people believed that in its winding length dwelt spirits, which they tried to propitiate,

(*Right*) When the Yellow River reaches the plains of Henan Province it becomes a wide turgid waterway, heavy with mud swept up from the loess-lands further upstream. From here to the sea 350 miles away the river is an east-west communication link for slow-moving cargo junks and, more importantly, the main source of irrigiation for a hundred million people's food supply. And whether the river threatens them with flood or drought depends on the snowfalls where the river rises on the roof of the world.

(*Above*) The ferry boat on the Yellow River carries the slogan 'Serve the People' reproduced from Chairman Mao's handwriting.

(*Right*) In the days before railways the only easy way of travelling between east and west China was by water, for China's main rivers, notably the Yellow and the Yangtze, rise in the west and flow eastwards. The Yellow River is navigable only in parts so the use of ferries and other passenger transport is limited. And because of danger of flooding until recent years, most big cities are set a few miles back from the banks.

(*Below*) North-south railway links span the river at Zhengzhou and elsewhere, connecting the southern city of Canton with the nation's capital, Peking. But the water has been known to rise above the bridges in times of very bad flooding and nowadays a special watch is kept along the river to mobilise commune work-forces when required to strengthen the levees.

The thin friable loess along the Yellow River is fertile but easily eroded and the streams in the loess-lands' countless deep ravines carry away the mud in the rainy season – away to the Yellow River and the sea. In very early times the climate of northern China was apparently warmer and more humid than it is today and much of it was covered with forests. Now it has been decided that the most effective way to keep the Yellow River from silting up is firstly by extensive terracing of the fields and secondly by an enormous programme of tree-planting to prevent the earth from being eroded. Afforestation has been underway for years and already the loess-lands are beginning to wear a different aspect, but the areas involved are vast and the work is far from finished. At one stage it was thought the problem had been solved when a huge dam with a reservoir behind it was built with Soviet help at the San Men Gorge. But the reservoir silted up and the dam had to be modified to let the mud through.

sometimes with human sacrifices. Later, imperial decrees demanded the building of dams to check the river in times of flood and reservoirs to store water for use when the river dried up. In this century American engineers working for China have drawn up elaborate plans for controlling the river. And since the early 1950s the communist government has embarked on a huge project – 46 dams along the river itself and 24 reservoirs along its main tributaries. The programme includes soil conservation and large-scale afforestation in the loess-lands, for if the erosion of the loess can be halted and the Yellow River cleansed of mud, the taming of the river would be brought within reach.

Visitors travelling along the river can witness the influence the waterway has had on the life and work of the nation. If they stop off at any of the museums in the cities that lie along its course, they can see the ancient China that excavations along its banks have uncovered; the priceless relics of the many dynasties that once flourished here – carvings, jewellery, procelain. And if they continue along the river's course, they can see modern China unfolding before their eyes: flourishing new cities, power-stations, irrigation projects. Along the Yellow River, China's great past and industrious present are displayed side by side.

Peking

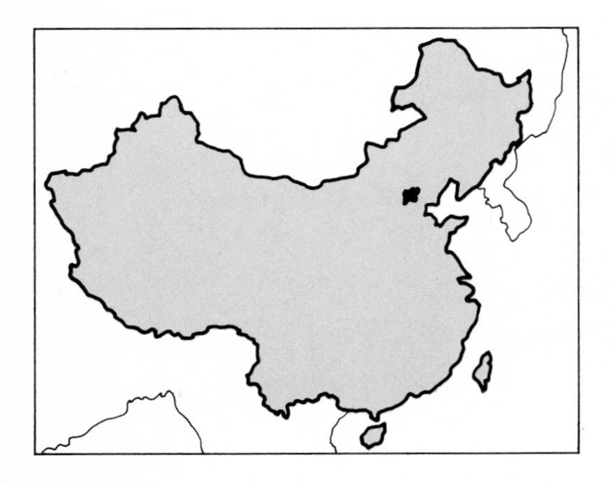

Peking is the capital of the world's most populous country. Behind the high grey walls of government ministries are decided the policies that shape the lives of nearly a billion Chinese people. The capital is an ancient city that has seen the rise and fall of many powerful emperors, invasions, popular uprisings and the creation and destruction of great palaces and works of art. It has for centuries been a centre of learning and political thought, and its universities have bred many notable literary and patriotic movements. Now Peking has also become an industrial centre, with a big iron and steel works and plants turning out machinery, textiles, chemicals, cameras and other goods. In modern China it is a national requirement that big cities must produce more than they consume.

The city administration looks after almost eight million people, nearly half of these within the actual city limits and the rest in the surrounding suburbs and communes. Despite the building of new estates, there is an acute housing shortage, as in nearly every large Chinese city. Yet the first impression that the visitor receives, riding in to Peking from the railway station or the new airport, is one of spaciousness. A wide boulevard, Chang An (Lasting Peace) Avenue – lined with hotels, ministries, museums and other public buildings – bisects the city from east to west. Traffic is heavy but consists almost entirely of lorries and bicycles; there are still few cars in China. Every family in Peking seems to own a bicycle – there must be about three million in the city.

In the heart of Peking, just south of the Forbidden City, the Temple of Heaven survives from ancient days as the symbolic meeting-place of God and Earth, with the Emperor as intercessor. A primitive temple has existed there since the very beginnings of Chinese civilization. It was the Emperor Yung Lo at the beginning of the Ming Dynasty (1368–1644) who built the present complex. Its most famous building is the architectural triumph known as the Hall of Prayer, rising to 99 feet, with pillars, walls and roof all of lacquered and gilt wood. South through two triple-arched gateways lies a smaller building, the Hall of Tablets, and beyond this is a triple-terraced circular altar of white stone, traditionally considered as the centre of the Universe, where the emperors sacrificed and prayed for good harvests.
The solemn rites were performed for the last time in December 1915 when army commander Yuan Shih-kai, claiming the imperial throne, drove to the Temple of Heaven in an armour-plated car.

In Peking's Forbidden City a huge courtyard fronts the Hall of Supreme Harmony, China's largest surviving palace building constructed entirely of wood. Downward-curving roofs of bright yellow glazed tiles – yellow was the colour reserved for emperors – tilt up at the eaves and are decorated with animal gargoyles. This hall was used only for the highest ceremonial occasions, such as the enthronement of a new emperor. The throne itself is flanked by columns of gold-painted dragons and dragons playing with pearls decorate the intricate ceiling. As the emperor took his seat, gongs and chimes of jade sounded from the gallery while the thick smoke of incense rose from bronze cranes, symbols of long life. Behind lie two more halls and the whole inner palace.

(*Above*) Near today's Summer Palace a few miles from Peking are the ruined sites of imperial retreats built centuries ago. The most famous Summer Palace of all was sacked in 1860 by French and British forces after the Chinese had ignored a new treaty giving more power to the Europeans and had murdered western prisoners.

(*Below*) Nearly 30 years later the Dowager Empress Ci Xi (Tz'u Hsi) decided to provide herself with a new Summer Palace, which was duly built on the site of a former imperial park around a lake. The cost was met by using funds badly needed for modernising the Navy – the only ship the Empress ordered to be built was the pleasure-house of stone on the Summer Palace's Kun Ming Lake.

(*Far right*) Most of these palace buildings are in an ornate, late nineteenth century style, but this four-storeyed pagoda dates back to the Ming Dynasty.

Halfway along Chang An Avenue lies the heart of Peking. This is the enormous Square of the Gate of Heavenly Peace (Tien An Men), big enough for more than a million people to assemble in it at one time. Here is the mausoleum of the late Chairman Mao Tse-tung; and here is the Heroes' Monument. On the west side is the Great Hall of the People, a huge heavy building in the Russian style, rushed to completion in ten months during the feverish days of the 1958 Great Leap Forward. On the north side stands the Gate of Heavenly Peace, from the top of which Chairman Mao proclaimed the setting up of the People's Republic on 1 October 1949.

Beyond the Gate, surrounded by high walls with towers, stretches a great complex of ceremonial halls, temples and palaces long known as the Forbidden City (today it is called the Palace Museum). This was the seat of the emperor, where he dwelt with his empress, concubines and hordes of eunuchs and officials. From here were issued the imperial edicts which all men must tremblingly obey. In the old days it was strictly forbidden for anyone outside the court and government even to approach the gates – for this was the imperial holy of holies.

The emperors of the Ming dynasty built the Forbidden City five and a half centuries ago after driving out the Mongols and destroying all their palaces. The visitor entering by the south gate steps into an enormous courtyard, on the other side of which stands the Hall of Supreme Harmony, a triumph of Chinese architecture with great roofs, carved doors and brilliant colours. More courtyards, halls of ceremony, imperial residences and museum-halls lie behind. The buildings and courtyards are arranged in strikingly harmonious proportion.

Architecturally, the Forbidden City is rivalled in Peking only by the Temple of Heaven, which lies due south. Here the emperor, in his role of intermediary between men and heaven, sacrificed at the winter and summer solstices and prayed for abundant harvests.

All that lies in the distant past. The Ming dynasty decayed, and its last emperor committed suicide on the hill behind his palace. The invading Manchus took over China in 1644 and ruled in their turn as the Qing (Ch'ing) dynasty. But they too became corrupt and decadent, and their last ruler, a young boy, lived, during the early years of this century, in curious isolation in the Forbidden City while officials sold off a substantial part of the dynasty's priceless historical relics and works of art.

(*Far left*) The buildings of the Summer Palace do not compare with the splendour of the Forbidden City in Peking. It is the calm lakeside landscape of the palace with its pavilions so attractively set on the hill slopes that makes it such an agreeable escape from the City.

(*Left*) The lake itself, which makes up more than three-quarters of the Summer Palace area, has an island joined to the mainland by a magnificent seventeen-arch bridge, dating back to the eighteenth century when the park was used by the famous Emperor Qian Long (Ch'ien Lung).

(*Left*) Few moon-gates remain in Peking, but they reveal a feature of old Chinese architecture in their representation of harmony and fulfilment. The gates are usually not entrances from the street but rather gateways into an inner courtyard, and were used not by strangers but only by family and close friends. For the women of the household it marked the limit of their domestic world, beyond which they were not allowed to venture. Until recently many Peking streets were lined with high walls ensuring privacy for the homes within which consisted of single-storeyed rooms surrounding the inner courtyard. Houses in Peking had to be single-storeyed because nobody could overlook the Forbidden City. Now most of these walled streets – hutongs – have been swept away and increasing numbers of Peking people live in housing blocks.

(*Above right*) Workmen carrying out restoration work on a gateway at the Summer Palace. The present Chinese Government spends large sums of money on maintaining and restoring ancient monuments, especially in the main cities. But many old buildings have fallen into disrepair or been swept away altogether to make room for industrial development or public housing, and during the so-called Cultural Revolution of the late sixties teenage 'rebels' carried out widespread damage and destruction. Some of this has since been repaired.

(*Below right*) Peking Opera is world famous. Traditionally its themes are taken from ancient Chinese classics and legends. In 'The Lady Generals of the Yang Clan' the women of the family carry on the war against the invader when all their men are killed. The banners sprouting from her shoulders show symbolically that the lady is a military commander. In recent years, more modern themes – resistance heroes, patriotic workers – had to figure exclusively but now older plays are coming back again.

Foreigners who lived in Peking in the days of the republic in the 1920s and '30s remember it as a picturesque city of charm and disconcerting contrasts. They recall the cries of street-sellers in the narrow high-walled lanes; the liveliness of the Thieves' Market that opened at midnight and closed at dawn; the wayside theatres; and the shopkeepers whose politeness and helpfulness were unrivalled throughout China. Much of this charm may have gone, but so has much that was deplorable. A Western diplomat's wife who knew the old days said recently that the biggest change she saw on returning to Peking today was that children no longer went barefoot in the snow.

Though many of the old shops have vanished, and antiques are not allowed to be exported, the restaurants of the city still flourish. The old Peking tradition of good food – especially Peking duck – is very much alive. The citizens are hearty eaters – they need to be in Peking's cold northern winters – and restaurants always seem to be crowded. At home, the staple diet is soup, vegetables, and cakes and rolls made of flour. Peking people, like other northerners, tend to eat wheat, whereas people from the south prefer rice.

There are other differences between north and south. Northerners tend to be taller and tougher than southerners, and they often have high cheekbones and straight noses. They also have the reputation of being straightforward and polite in their approach, with a lively sense of humour. But these days such regional distinctions are lost in Peking, as thousands of workers flood into the capital from other parts of China. Now in Peking's streets you hear the accents of many provinces. (However, for all those Chinese who do not work in Peking or have no family there, it is very difficult to obtain permission even to visit the city, let alone live there.)

Construction work, already a major activity, is being further expanded. There are plans to build more modern hotels (as joint ventures with foreign firms), to accommodate an expected flood of tourists. The administration has renovated the airport and built new housing estates. There are plans to extend the underground railway – the only one in China – which runs from the city centre out to the Western Hills. The underground is connected to an elaborate system of air-raid shelters built – as the guides tell travellers – as a defence against any attack by aggressive powers, especially the 'Soviet imperialists'.

Peking people agree that their material conditions are generally of a higher standard than in other Chinese cities. Consumer goods are more plentiful; there is a greater choice of food and more meat. The capital holds a privileged position.

(*Below*) The famous road from Peking to the tombs north of the city where thirteen of the emperors of the Ming Dynasty lie buried. It was the Ming Emperor Yung Lo who built the Forbidden City which remains today and he also chose the site of the tombs. The approach road is two-thirds of a mile long and lined with eighteen pairs of statues of men and animals. Along this road passed the solemn funeral processions, including faithful eunuchs who followed the emperor to death and were buried near him.

(*Right*) More consumer goods than ever before are on sale in the department stores of Peking, though a TV set may cost a worker six months' wages and most are bought by factories or clubs for communal viewing. Peking was once a centre of government, literature and learning. It is still the administrative capital and a university centre but it is also an industrial city turning out machine tools, farming equipment, textiles and a wide range of consumer goods, providing jobs for millions of workers.

(*Left*) On a former site of an old market they now assemble trucks in one of Peking's newest car factories. Peking has lost much of its old-fashioned charm but it has joined the twentieth century.

(*Below*) A mighty human spectacular to mark the opening of China's National Games, under a vast benign head of Chairman Mao. China is making great efforts to enter and impress the international sports world, but the face of the Chairman is seen less often as China follows more pragmatic policies.

The Northern Plains

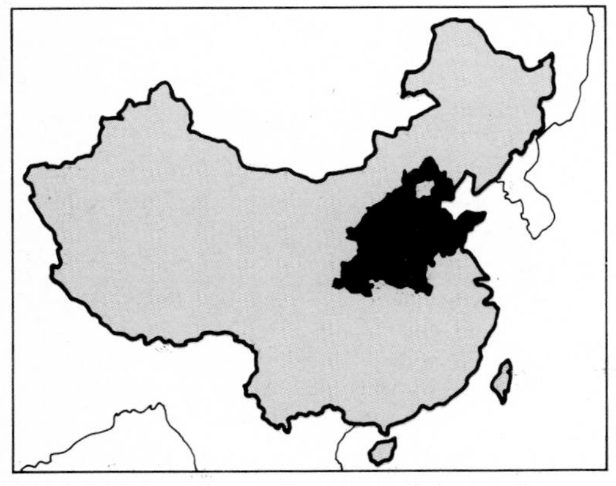

(*Right*) Thirty-five miles east of the ancient city of Xian is a pleasant hillside with hot springs much favoured by past emperors. They built a palace with pavilions and pleasure-gardens called 'Hua Qing Gong', the 'Palace of Glorious Purity'. The Tang emperor Xuan Zong (713–755 AD) used to come here with his concubine, the beautiful Yang Gui Fei and no one else was allowed to enjoy the hot springs. After his death the palace fell into disrepair but much was restored during the Qing Dynasty (1644–1911), including this lovely 'Pavilion of Rosy Sunset'.

(*Below*) The farm production brigade at Dazhai was always held up as the supreme example of hard work and organization triumphing over steep and stony soil. When drought hit northern China in 1977 they all carried water a mile uphill to save the crops. Dazhai's achievements are still praised, but nowadays China is looking more to modern farming methods, including greater use of fertilizers, to solve the food problem.

Travellers leaving the forests and steel centres of Manchuria to come south across the Great Wall into China's Northern Plains find themselves in a land of great farms of wheat and cotton, ancient and modern cities, railways leading to all parts of China – and scores of millions of people.

This is the area sometimes called the Lower Yellow River Region. It includes the provinces of Hebei (Hopei), Shandong, Shanxi, Shaanxi (Shensi) and Henan (Honan) – and most important of all, China's great capital, Peking.

This region saw the unfolding of much of China's early history, for here were the capitals of the ancient kingdoms that intrigued and fought before China was unified into one empire. Here, too, for thousands of years, hard-working Chinese families have been cultivating the alluvial soil brought down by mighty rivers like the Yellow, the Hai, the Huai and the Yangtze. In some parts of the region several thousand people wrest a living from each square mile – an area which in Europe might support a dozen families at most. Life is organized collectively, in people's communes, whose basic units are the original villages, now called production teams.

This is a region where the western foreigner made his presence fleetingly felt in pre-war days; the industrial city of Tianjin (Tientsin), 75 miles southeast of Peking, once provided concession areas for foreign governments, and West European architecture – churches and residential areas – still strikes a curiously alien note. Tianjin, which has a population of nearly 4 million, is now one of China's main industrial and commercial centres, possessing textile and flour mills, chemical and machine-building works and a port capable of taking ships of 11,000 tons.

A hundred miles east of Tianjin lies the industrial centre of Tangshan, on the Harbin-Peking railway. It grew rapidly following the opening up of the nearby Kailuan coal mines towards the end of the last century. Besides coal, Tangshan is famous for its iron and steel, ceramics, locomotives, textiles and pharmaceuticals. The city suffered terrible losses in the devastating earthquakes of 1976, and reconstruction is still going on. It is said that, by sheerest chance, shifts working underground in the coal mines were unaffected by the heavy tremors which reduced most buildings to rubble.

In former times when foreigners and rich Chinese wanted to get away from the dust and bustle of the cities of Hebei province, they would make for the little seaside resort of Beidaihe (Peitaiho), with its charming small hotels and beaches and donkey-rides for children. It is still a resort today, very popular with diplomats and their families stationed in Peking, and still retains much of its old atmosphere.

To see the new world, the world of the future, you must travel a few hundred miles across the Northern Plains to the Taihang Mountains southwest of Peking, where the Dazhai (Tachai) farming production brigade in Xiyang (Hsiyang) County is famous as China's pace-setter in agriculture. This brigade was once an impoverished hill village with poor soil and wretched harvests. But in the past 20 years it has been transformed by collective effort into a model village with high yields – and one modern Chinese slogan is 'In agriculture, learn from Tachai!'

South of the province of Shanxi stretches that of Henan, which means South of the River – and any reference to a river in Chinese place names is nearly always, as here, to the Yellow River. Along its tributaries in Henan province stand the cities that were once China's ancient capitals: Luoyang, Zhengzhou, Kaifeng. They have undergone profound changes in recent years.

Although Luoyang is still famous for its wonderful show of peonies in the parks each April (about which poets were writing a thousand years ago), it is now a great industrial centre, with a tractor factory employing 30,000 workers. Of the historical relics unearthed in Luoyang, a fraction are displayed in the local museum to recall the days when this was the capital of the Chou, Han and eastern T'ang dynasties. The T'ang Empress Wu once built what was probably China's biggest pagoda in Luoyang; it was later burned down. The empress also had a gigantic Buddha carved in the famous grotto temple of Lung-men about eight miles south of Luoyang. There are altogether more than 2,000 grottoes and niches in the cliffs of this area, containing about 100,000 Buddhist statues and images, and more than 3,500 inscriptions and carved stone tablets.

In Zhengzhou, when construction workers were removing part of the old city wall to lay out a new street, they came across the remains of a city of the Shang dynasty, more than 3,000 years old. Today Zhengzhou is a large railway junction and textile centre with a population of three quarters of a million. Southwest of the city lies the Shao Lin temple, whose monks developed the style of wrestling now known all over the world as Kung Fu. The temple's ancient halls were badly burned during civil conflict in 1926 – another example of the widespread damage or destruction of the relics of China's long and rich history.

(Above) The great land mass of China (nine and a half million square kilometres) has a continental climate which means that the summers – short in the north and long in the south – are always hot. So if your house is small and crowded the natural thing is to sleep in the open. In the cities, parks are often left open all night in the hot weather.

(Far left) Buddhism spread through China from 500 AD – about the same time as Christianity was being accepted throughout Europe. Chinese Buddhists often retained belief in their other two philosophies – Taoism and Confucianism. The Buddhist doctrine of compassion for human suffering found an eager audience in the Chinese masses. Later Buddhists were to have secular power: monasteries were banking centres and priests influenced emperors. This follower of Buddha, or Bodisattra, is Hsuan Chung-su who was revered as a legendary warrior, and chief of 32 heavenly generals.

(Below left) A simple home in Datong city in Shanxi province. For thousands of years the Chinese have kept song-birds for company, taking them on walks and to tea-houses. In recent years song-birds were frowned on as useless food consumers, but now they are permitted again and seen in city parks and streets.

(*Above*) This ancient monastery gateway near Taiyuan in Shanxi province has survived centuries of storms and stress, for Taiyuan lies directly in the path of armies invading from the North. To pay for China's defence emperors levied heavy taxes on monasteries, which brought loss of political and financial power to Chinese Buddhism but improved its spiritual standing in the eyes of the people.

At the end of the 19th century, when China's last imperial dynasty, the Qing, was being weakened by Western incursions, the famous Summer Palace in Peking was sacked and many Chinese treasures were lost abroad. Then the Japanese invasion of World War Two and the civil war that followed both caused further destruction of the heritage of China's past. But long before that, in ancient times, whenever a new dynasty seized power in China it often burnt down the palaces of the old regime.

The greatest dynasty in China's history was the T'ang (618-906). At its height it rivalled, in the flowering of literature and the arts, the Renaissance in Europe. Its capital, Chang An, was near present-day Xian in Shaanxi province, not far from the Yellow River. Its palace and gardens were immortalized by China's greatest poets, but no trace of them remains today.

Most of the relics of China's past civilizations that have survived have done so through having been buried. Excavations of the tombs of emperors and princes have yielded enormous quantities of art treasures – priceless T'ang carvings, figurines, lapis lazuli, gold, porcelain, jade (which the Chinese thought had the virtue of saving the dead from decay), and objects of daily use that the dead might need in the next world. A few years ago, near Xian, archaeologists began uncovering the tomb of the Ch'in emperor Shih Huang Ti, who first united China in the 3rd century BC. The excavations revealed 6,000 life-size terracotta figures of men-at-arms and cavalry horses, buried to guard their dead lord. They are works of great craftsmanship, all modelled to show their individual character.

As China presses on with the modernization of its farms, the digging of wells and irrigation channels leads to the continual uncovering of more relics of the past. What has been excavated so far in east China alone must constitute only a small fraction of all the surviving treasures and art-objects, most of which still lie buried in tombs and the foundations of destroyed palaces and cities. The present Chinese government has allocated large funds for archaeological pro-

(*Above*) This experienced woman worker is teaching oxyacetylene welding to a new comrade at one of the big new factories at Zhengzhou near the Yellow River. An ancient and for long neglected town Zhengzhou was given new life by the railways and now has 750,000 people instead of the 100,000 of thirty years ago. They make farm tools, electrical equipment and machines for the textile industry in northern China.

jects to uncover these treasures and for the preservation of ancient monuments and the restoration of Buddhist cave temples.

War may destroy the monuments of man but it cannot disturb those of Nature. From the level plain of Shandong province Mount Tai rises abruptly in a series of wildly beautiful peaks. Emperors through the centuries journeyed to this 'First of the Five Sacred Mountains' to pray to heaven, and it has long since lodged itself in the general Chinese consciousness: 'To have eyes and not see Mount Tai' is a Chinese way of describing ignorance; and, in talking of the impact of death, the historian Sima Qian said, 'It may be weightier than Mount Tai or lighter than a feather.'

The Taishan temple at the foot of the mountain comprises about 35 square miles of pavilions and towers, tall pines and cypresses and stone tablets. The main hall is one of China's three great ancient palace-style buildings – the others being the Hall of Supreme Harmony in Peking's Forbidden City, and the Confucian Temple at Chu Fu, the sage's birthplace, which lies a short distance north of Mount Tai, on the way to Jinan (Tsinan), the capital of Shandong.

Jinan, a bustling city with more than a million people, has a history dating back at least 2,600 years. It is often called the 'City of Springs' because of the 100 and more natural springs which bubble out of the ground within the city limits.

The present is laying an impatient hand on the ancient countryside of the Northern Plains, as China's programme of modernization gets underway: hundreds of miles of railways to be laid down, harbours to be dredged and deepened, roadways to be extended, steelworks and chemical plants to be set up, and, above all, more fertilizer plants to be built, to help produce the food needed for an ever-increasing population.

The Yungang Grottoes near Datong, northern Shanxi province are one of the earliest and most impressive groups of rock sculpture in China. Work started around 460 AD under emperors of the Wei people who had come down from the North but adopted Chinese ways and became Buddhists. Extensions went on until 494 AD. There are some 51,000 sculptured figures remaining, the largest 17 metres high and the smallest two centimetres, in 53 caves distributed over more than half a mile of hills. In 1973 the later Premier Chou En-lai visited the grottoes with President Pompidou of France and ordered restoration work to be carried out, at a cost of more than a million yuan. A rich coal seam running underneath the grottoes has been left untouched.

Tibet

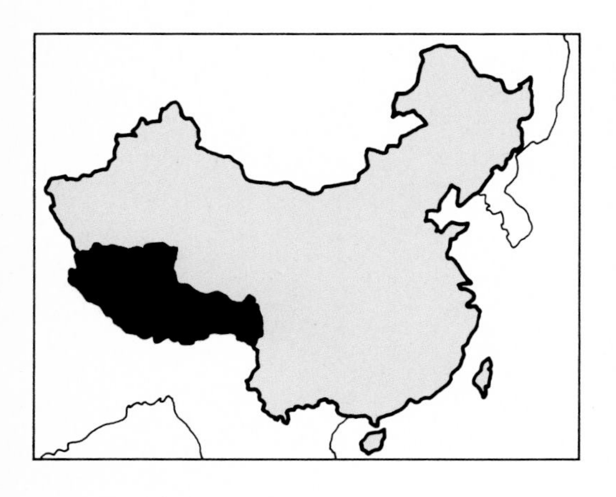

Tibet is the land of the world's highest mountains. Massive ranges guard it to the north, west and south. North lies the Kun-lun range, reaching heights of 16-22,000 ft, while south are the Himalayas, towering to a maximum of 29,000 ft at Mount Everest on the border with Nepal. Lesser mountain ranges cross the region itself, and even the general level of the lowest central part of Tibet averages about 14,000 ft above sea-level.

Although eastern Tibet does not have quite such high mountains as the north, west and south, it is so barren and remote that it is almost as inaccessible as the rest of the province. Until the 1950s the land journey from Peking to Lhasa, the capital of Tibet, would normally take more than six months.

The northern half of Tibet is a high wilderness, where the icy winds are so strong that snow settles only in the upland valleys, and human beings find it practically impossible to survive. The only animals that can exist here are the wild yak and antelope and the wolves that live on them. Hunters sometimes visit the area; otherwise it is a daunting emptiness on the roof of the world.

Immediately south is a large area of upland lakes, mountains and sparse grazing lands, where sturdy nomadic groups of herdsmen live in tents and tend yak, sheep and goats.

(*Right*) The Himalayas (home of the gods according to Indian tradition) are the highest mountains in the world and the barrier between India and the Chinese People's Republic. The Chinese claim that Mount Everest, the world's highest peak – they call it Chololangma – is partly in Chinese territory.

(*Far right*) Southern Tibet is relatively sheltered from the icy winds of the northern plateau. Former manor houses now used for communal purposes survive on the lower mountain slopes, with glaciers far above.

(*Above*) The Tibetan plateau is one of China's five biggest pastoral areas, covering thousands of square miles, but the wind and cold are fierce especially at higher altitudes. It takes the yak (the long-haired humped Tibetan ox) and the leathery Tibetan herdsman to support the climate and survive.

The most southerly quarter of Tibet consists of the high valleys of such well-known rivers as the Brahmaputra (which the Tibetans call the Tsangpo), the Salween, the Mekong and the Yangtze. Here lie Tibet's agricultural lands and here live most of its 2 million inhabitants.

The Tibetans, no longer an independent nation but now simply a minority group within the Chinese People's Republic, are a vigorous people, handsome, high cheek-boned and cheerful. Once, when they were a mighty nation, every year, as soon as the harvest was in, their armies spread into China. On one occasion they even occupied the Chinese capital at Xian in the north.

From about the 6th century, Tibet became a great Buddhist centre. It inherited the entire legacy of Indian Buddhism and its manifold teachings at a time when India and many other countries had given up the religion under the pressures of Islam, and its missionaries spread the Buddhist gospel as far north as Mongolia. Tibetan monasteries (the first was built about 750) were colleges of Buddhist scripture and remained so, with their thousands of monks and followers, for 1,200 years, until 1959 when China took over Tibet and began the process of ousting Buddhism in favour of communism. But the influence of Tibetan Buddhism still remains strong in neighbouring Nepal, Bhutan and Sikkim, India.

Far back in China's history Tibetan lamas (monks) exerted great influence over the Mongol emperors, who were ready to favour the religion most likely to help and protect them. When the lamas visited Peking, they had to compete with Muslims, Taoists and Christian Jesuits in argument and tests of magic. Marco Polo writes that the arts of the Tibetan lamas, which could cause the emperor's cup to rise from the ground to his mouth, convinced him that their Buddhism was superior to Christianity.

For centuries Tibet was left undisturbed. Then came the setting up of the People's Republic in China and, not many years later, the arrival in Lhasa of units of the Chinese People's Liberation Army and hordes of officials. Their task has been to drive home to the Tibetans that their land is now part of China and that they will receive their share of the benefits of socialist administration and progress. Now China allows foreigners to visit Tibet, the last province to be

(*Above*) The written Tibetan language was formerly entirely religious. Since the Chinese communists took over efforts have been made to modernise the language and include words needed to express modern concepts – atoms, aircraft, biochemistry, communism. Literacy is spreading through the countryside. But the Han (standard Chinese) language is taught and used for higher education. Tibetan students attending universities use the standard Chinese language.

adapted to the system of people's communes.

The Chinese claim that Tibet has largely been changed for the better, that education is now widespread, that corrupt monasteries have been closed and monks have been obliged to earn their living on the land, and that, despite reports of continued resistance, especially by the nomadic herdsmen, the bulk of the Tibetan people are enthusiastically behind the new regime.

Today the capital, Lhasa, has 100,000 inhabitants – three times as many as 20 years ago – and is becoming an industrial city, with a coal mine and 29 factories. However, ancient monuments are being preserved, among them the Potala, former palace of the Dalai Lamas (once heads of the Buddhist Church and rulers of Tibet) – a huge complex of buildings 13 storeys high that seems to float mysteriously on the hill-slopes above the city.

East of the Potala the gilt-tiled Jolgkhang Temple covers 215,000 square feet of land. A willow enclosed in a wall before the gate is said to have been planted by Princess Wen Cheng of China's T'ang Dynasty when she came to marry King Song-tzan Gampo of Tibet about 1,300 years ago.

The communists are not merely preserving Tibetan palaces and temples but restoring them so that they can be open to the public, which visits them in hundreds every day.

Eastern Tibet is becoming increasingly industrialized and factories line both sides of the Nyang River, now spanned by the August the First Bridge. A new match factory, as well as paper and woollen mills, a hospital and a number of schools, have all been built in recent years. Most of this is due to the large number of technicians who have arrived from other parts of China to supervise planning and construction.

(*Right above and below*) For Europeans Tibet was for many centuries a forbidden land until a British force fought its way through the high mountains to the capital Lhasa in 1904 and entered the Potala, palace of the Dalai Lama. 'A vast and entrancing panorama,' was how an expedition member described it, 'crowned by golden pavilions, with great stairways and buttressing walls sixty feet high.' When the Tibetan rebels resisted the communist presence in 1959 they made the Potala and the adjoining Jolgkhang Temple their headquarters.

(*Far right*) Monasteries and temples against a background of mountains still dominate the Lhasa scene. Twenty years ago nearly a quarter of all adult males in Tibet were lamas (Buddhist monks) living in more than 2,500 monasteries. For centuries Lhasa had been the religious centre of the world for vast numbers of Buddhists in Mongolia, Bhutan, Nepal and several Chinese provinces. It was a great picturesque dirty city accommodating a floating population of pilgrims. Nowadays the communists claim that, thanks to education, modern hygiene and the abolition of serfdom, Tibet is fast joining the twentieth century. Lamaism is no longer an effective force. But it will still take time for the Tibetans to adapt to collective reforms imposed from outside.

The Yangtze River

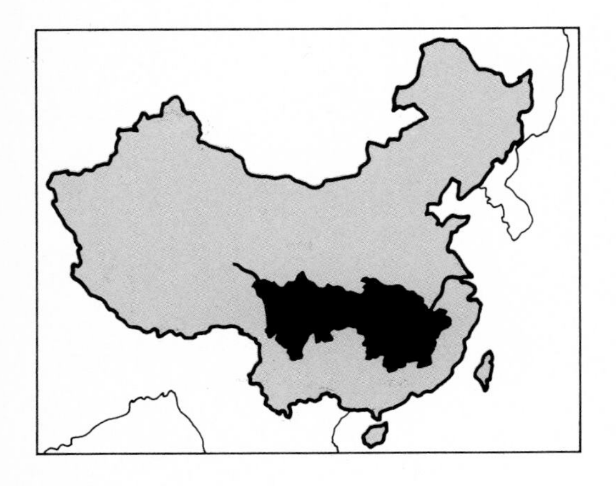

(*Right*) The boats of the Yangtze River vary enormously in rig and tonnage. In the three Great Gorges to the east of Sichuan the cargo and passenger steamers are high powered and strong hulled to fight the treacherous waters. Nearer the sea, in the long stretches downstream from Nanking, they use the tall-sailed square-rigged river junks to catch the lightest breeze moving over the broad river.

(*Below*) This is a land of abundant rice, which is often mixed into noodle form (like macaroni) and dries along the riverside in the open air. The Chinese saying is that if there are good harvests in the Yangtze provinces of Hubei and Hunan, as well as in Guangdong province to the south, then all of China will be well fed.

Eastward from mountainous Tibet lies one of the most fertile valleys of all China, the central Red Valley in the ancient province of Sichuan (Szechuan), whose name means 'Four Rivers'.

The known history of Sichuan goes back at least 2,000 years. It always remained somehow apart from the rest of China, and in the 3rd century, when the country was split into three kingdoms, Sichuan (or the Kingdom of Shu, as it was then known) survived gloriously against its enemies. This was partly due to the great cunning of its chief minister, Zhu Ge Liang – to whom was dedicated a temple that survives to this day – and partly to the natural defence of the high mountains almost surrounding the province. An old saying runs: 'How hard the road to Shu is, hard as the road to Heaven.'

Through Sichuan, through thousands of miles of farmlands and rice-paddies, through towering gorges, and on to the Pacific, flows the Yangtze, the longest river in China. Along it and its many tributaries lives the greatest concentration of China's people.

The river rises in the high mountain wastes of Tibet. Only in recent years have exploration teams found that the exact location of its source is several hundred miles further west than the place previously given. So the mighty river is now known to have a total length of about 4,000 miles, which makes it the fourth longest river in the world.

The Yangtze flows through China's history, through the lives of scholars, warriors, emperors and their famous mistresses, and untold millions of hard-working peasant families. 'Thoughts Written While Travelling at Night' by the famous poet Du Fu came to his mind while he was voyaging down the Yangtze across the great eastern plains. Legend says that an emperor of the Han dynasty once shot a dragon in the river. And Mao Tse-tung set off a keep-fit campaign by swimming across it.

The river bears various names. Near the source they call it the Tuotuo; in the high mountains of Qinghai province it's the Tongtian (Tungtien); roaring down through foaming gorges to Sichuan it becomes the Jinsha – River of Golden Sands. In the Tiger Leap Gorge, 7½ miles long and flanked by moun-

(*Above*) The city of Chongqing is a busy inland port and industrial centre spread over steep hills where the Jia Ling River flows into the Yangtze in Sichuan province. From the upper city flights of steps lead down past the site of the former city walls to the waterside far below. Chongqing is the traffic centre for the whole of prosperous Sichuan and for trade between Tibet and the South-West and the rest of China. The Chinese government and many universities were evacuated here during the Japanese wartime invasion.

tains 10,000 feet high, the river twists and turns in large sweeping bends, and here rice crops and plantains flourish and the air is filled with the scent of wild olives. Further on, gold has been found in the river's sands, and iron and nickel in the hills near by.

At Yibin (Yipin) in Sichuan the river leaves the high mountains and snakes along the southern edge of the fertile Sichuan plain, where it passes through minor gorges and washes the walls of Chongqing (Chungking) and other cities that lie at the mouths of tributaries. These minor rivers swell the waters of the Yangtze as it then moves on eastward towards the Three Gorges, which have been called the throat of the Yangtze. Their steep rock faces often tower thousands of feet to the sky, so that in some places the gorges see no sun until noon.

Thirty years ago junks and steamers moving upstream had to depend on winching or human haulage to negotiate the more difficult shoals and turns. Teams of hundreds of men toiled along the haulage ways, harnessed with ropes and urged on with cries and gongs. Drownings and wrecks were frequent. Gradually schemes of improvement were carried out. In the 1950s and '60s more than a hundred shoals were dredged from the channel – about 5 million cubic yards of rock and stone. Signal stations with lighting systems now make the river safe for night navigation.

To voyage by river steamer along this stretch of the river, between Chongqing and the central Yangtze, is to make one of the most fascinating journeys any traveller can wish for in China. The atmosphere is humid, and the sun breaking through the mists and thin spray often creates rainbow effects which contrast strikingly with the grey expanse of sheer cliff. Chinese historians say that during what is known as the Spring and Autumn Period – 770-476 BC – the Yangtze River flowed out from the Three Gorges only to lose itself in a huge expanse of swampland – the 'Marshes of Cloud and Dream'. But since then the pressures of current brought about by four other rivers joining the great water-

(*Above*) Thousands of tons of goods are transported in and out of Chongqing every day by river-boats such as these. And for many thousands of river families they represent home and shelter. But the busy scene on the Yangtze at Chongqing also includes big sailing junks with long oars and many river steamers. The drawback of Chongqing is its climate – hot and humid. Relief is in the neighbouring hills where ancient temples and Buddhas survive in the forests.

way have resulted in changes to the marshland and formed the enormous Dongting (Tungting) Lake on its southern side, in Hunan province.

Both the river and lake in this area pose a seasonal threat of severe flooding to the surrounding farmland, and to prevent this, the government has set up five major flood retention and reclamation zones round the lake, together with flood diversion zones for use in emergencies.

The fight against floods is never-ending. The lower reaches of all China's great rivers are likely to overflow under the pressure of tons of water from the melting glaciers and snows of the Tibetan mountains. Every year armies of workers and peasants strengthen and raise the dykes, but every year the rivers bring down more silt and mud, raising the river-beds higher again and threatening the dykes.

Past the Dongting Lake, 150 miles further on, the flourishing city of Wuhan has suffered heavy losses from Yangtze floods. In 1931 the city was submerged and 30,000 people were drowned, and in 1954 there was further severe flooding. Wuhan is a vital Chinese communications link by both river and land. It is also famous as the place where in 1911 the revolution broke out that was to sweep away imperial rule and lead to the setting up of a republic.

Many plans have been drawn up to divert the waters of the Yangtze northward, in order to relieve the pressure on the lower reaches and to provide much-needed irrigation to northern areas.

The provinces of Hubei and Hunan, right in the centre of China, are the lands of the country's richest rice harvests. One great plain of rich soil, watered by meandering streams, stretches for several hundred miles north and south of the Dongting Lake. The West would call this a land of milk and honey; the Chinese call it 'The Land of Rice and Fish'. Besides food, the provinces grow cotton and tea. Central Hubei is one of the biggest cotton-growing areas in the whole country, and the tea plantations in the hills to the south are vast.

The millions of tons of water the Yangtze brings down from the snows of Tibet swell the volume of the huge Dongting Lake and overflow across the ricefields of Hunan – a familiar ingredient in the lives of central Chinese. Living with the Yangtze means weeks of hard labour repairing banks and dams. It also means Dragon Boat races along the river, ostensibly to preserve the memory of a righteous but wronged minister but possibly connected with much older ceremonies to placate the river god and make him look benevolently on the fields, sparing them flood and drought. For that even human sacrifice was justified. Nowadays conservancy schemes are yielding results, but the Chinese farmers are still acutely conscious of the power of their great rivers to bring prosperity or disaster.

(Right) You can meet a man like this in the streets of Nanking, Peking, Canton or any Chinese city. He has the patient, wide-awake look and lurking sense of humour common to most Chinese. He may be an illiterate villager working in a town factory. He may be the highly cultured last survivor of some great family come down in the world. But he has this in common with millions of Chinese of his generation – he has seen wars, floods, famines, revolution and the rise and fall of the great.

(Far right above) Centuries of farming have changed the contours of vast areas of China's land. In the great river valleys intricate systems of irrigation have been developed, moving the water by pumps and paddle-wheels from one field or terrace to the next. Until now the Chinese farmers have been rich in work force but short on fertilizer, and yield per acre is still less than in Japan or Australia. Now farming is to have top priority in China's modernization programmes.

(Far right below) This is the farm at Shaoshan, near Changsha in Hunan, where Mao Tse-tung was born on the 26 December 1893. The buildings show that Mao's parents were fairly affluent farmers. Quarrels were frequent between young Mao and his tough ex-soldier father. His mother, a gentle Buddhist, often served as peacemaker. Now the farm is preserved as a place of pilgrimage.

It was in Hunan province, on a farm near the village of Shaoshan, that Mao Tse-tung was born in 1893; and he went to school at the provincial capital, Changsha.

On the eastern borders of Hunan province stretch the Jing Gang (Chingkang) Mountains, difficult of access, joining Hunan with the province of Jiangxi (Kiangsi). The communists set up their revolutionary base in these mountains after their organization in Shanghai and other cities was broken by the Nationalist government in 1927. And, after resisting repeated attacks by the Nationalist armies on their stronghold, it was from the mountains that the communists started out on their Long March across China until they found security and the chance to re-group in the north, near the Yellow River.

In the northeast of Jiangxi is China's biggest freshwater lake, the Poyang Lake, and near this lies the provincial capital, Nanchang, famous as the birthplace of the People's Liberation Army in 1927.

Across the border in Anhui rise the Huang Mountains, whose variety of scenery the Chinese claim to be unrivalled. They offer a landscape of high peaks, rocks, pines and rhododendrons, surmounted by changing cloud effects, often painted by Chinese artists. The highest of the 72 peaks reaches to 1,800 metres (nearly 6,000 feet) and consists of grotesquely shaped rocks separated by deep, narrow ravines often hidden by mist. Pines grow out of rock crevices in strange forms, some hanging upside down, some spreading horizontally. At the foot of the mountains are hot springs.

(*Right*) The great river bridge at Nanking is the third built across the Yangtze – the others are at Wuhan and Chongqing. It is double-decked with the railway below and an eight lane highway overhead and was completed in December 1968. At this point the Yangtze is about 1,000 metres wide, the stream is deep and fast-moving and the soil of the river bed very varied. The Chinese consider the bridge a national engineering triumph.

(*Below*) All the emperors of the great Ming dynasty are buried near Peking with the exception of the first, Zhu Yuan Zhang (Chu Yuan-chang) who was buried south of the Zi Jin Shan (Purple and Gold Mountain) east of Nanking. The original Ming tomb was very splendid but 600 years later all that survives is the entrance avenue of stone animals and men.

(Above) On Nanking's eastern outskirts near the Ming tomb is the mausoleum of Dr Sun Yatsen, revered as founder of the Republic in 1912 after the overthrow of China's last imperial dynasty. Dr Sun died in 1925 and his body was brought here from Peking when the mausoleum was completed four years later.

Mountains occupy a special place in the minds of the Chinese; they represent peace and solitude and freedom from the corrupting restlessness of the world of the plains. Mount Jiuhua (Chiuhua), overlooking the Yangtze near the ancient town of Wuhu, is one of China's four famous Buddhist sacred mountains. The monasteries among its high forests contain more than 1,300 ancient documents, seals, fine pieces of calligraphy, paintings and Buddhist scriptures. The poet Du Fu was entranced by the mountain's 99 peaks and its caves, cataracts and ancient trees. He compared its shape to that of a cluster of nine lotus flowers, and it was thus that the mountain acquired its name, which means nine flowers.

By the time the Yangtze reaches the great city of Nanking, it is a broad flood, a huge natural barrier between south and north China. Nanking has had its full share of floods, wars and rebellions, but more of the past has survived here than in many other great cities. The Chunghua Gate, built in the early years of the Ming dynasty (1368-1644), is the largest gateway in China; its three enclosures can hold 3,000 men. A more modern monument of interest is the mausoleum of Sun Yat Sen, founder of the republic that replaced the rule of the emperors in the early years of this century.

Nanking has always been a centre of Chinese culture and learning, and great poets, calligraphers, mathematicians and painters have settled here in the past. Today, although increasingly industrialized, the city retains its many institutes of higher learning.

After Nanking, the Yangtze enters its last stretch of 200 miles, to the East China Sea, meandering through the fertile countryside of the broad coastal plain. As it nears its journey's end, its width increases to more than 45 miles to form a trumpet-shaped estuary more than 120 miles long.

Shanghai

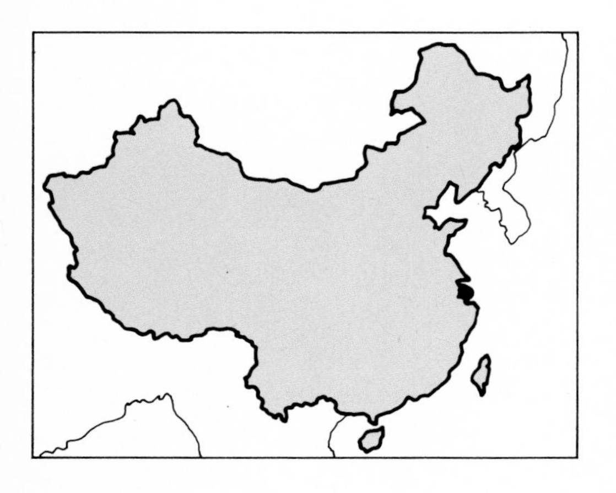

Shanghai, with an estimated population of 11 million, is the largest city in the world – bigger even than Tokyo. It is a city with its own unique atmosphere and personality. It lacks the formality and discipline of the capital, Peking, but possesses a dynamism and independence that stem from its mercantile, international, wheeler-dealing past. Its history encompasses privation and suffering, great prosperity, revolution and war, thriving art and literature, international banking and business and communist politics.

It was in an unoccupied girls' school in Shanghai that the Chinese Communist Party was founded in 1921. In later years Chairman Mao used Shanghai as a base for launching attacks on his party rivals when he found that they were becoming too well organized in Peking. And in World War Two Shanghai was the scene of heroic fighting by the Chinese troops against the invading Japanese, who finally took the city and held it throughout the war.

The Shanghai of today is a relatively new city. It began as a small fishing village in the Middle Ages and later, because of its position near the mouth of the Yangtze River, developed into a port and trading centre. The great change came when, in 1842, the British defeated the Chinese in the Opium Wars and Shanghai became one of the first so-called treaty ports, through which China was obliged to open up trade contacts with the West on a large scale.

Foreign settlements were established in the city (there were 13 of them by the 1930s) and enjoyed extra-territorial status, exempt from Chinese law. Most were grouped together in one international settlement where British influence predominated, but the French had their separate concession, known locally as Frenchtown. Around the settlements lay Chinese Shanghai, which covered the whole spectrum from wealth to poverty – streets of luxurious, secluded houses, filthy areas of small workshops that employed children, and slums in whose streets people died from hunger and privation.

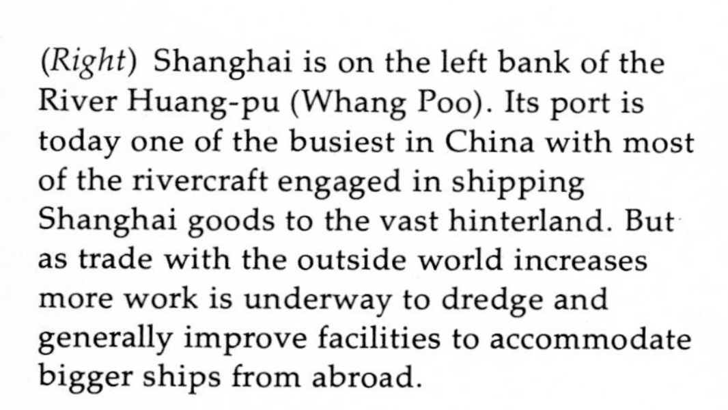

(*Right*) Shanghai is on the left bank of the River Huang-pu (Whang Poo). Its port is today one of the busiest in China with most of the rivercraft engaged in shipping Shanghai goods to the vast hinterland. But as trade with the outside world increases more work is underway to dredge and generally improve facilities to accommodate bigger ships from abroad.

(*Far right*) From a high building the view south across Soochow Creek takes in the famous Bund – with the former British consulate, now part of a seamen's club, in the foreground, and behind it the buildings that once housed foreign banks, a great hotel and a luxurious western club. All that atmosphere of entrepreneurial wealth and business ended with the communist take-over.

(*Above*) The high office block known as 'Shanghai Mansion' near the bridge over Soochow Creek. The creek flows under the bridge into the Huang-pu (Whang-poo) River and 14 miles northeast of Shanghai the Huang-pu empties into the Yangtze estuary. When the communists first came to power, the port of Shanghai became a dead stretch of waterfront for some years with only a few foreign ships visiting every week. Now trade with the outside world is expanding vigorously.

By the turn of the century Shanghai had become a great centre of foreign business and industrialization and had acquired the glittering image of a cosmopolitan city where enterprising foreigners – and Chinese – could make enormous fortunes. One of the early foreign arrivals was the company of Jardine Matheson, which had enriched itself through the opium trade and now launched into textiles, banking and many other activities. A later arrival, Sir Victor Sassoon, built the great Cathay Hotel (now the Friendship Hotel) on the waterfront.

A sinister force to be reckoned with for many years in Shanghai was Tu Yueh-sen, a fruit pedlar from the city streets who fought his way to the leadership of the feared secret society the Green Dragons, which controlled all drug trafficking. In the days before World War Two, Shanghai was notorious not only for drugs but for large-scale gambling and prostitution. It was also a place where foreign seamen got 'shanghaied' (drugged and press-ganged) and a planning headquarters for piracy along the Chinese coast. Paradoxically, it was also a great centre of Western missionary work. American missionary funds enabled the famous St John's University to be established. But the most important role Shanghai played for the Chinese themselves was that it brought them face-to-face with the great world of Western commerce. From all over China, from small towns and impoverished villages, men came to Shanghai to seek their fortunes, to try their luck and skill in business.

Since those restless days, Shanghai has undergone sweeping changes. The foreigners now come only as visitors, the old world of luxury and entertainment has vanished. Many of the same buildings along the famous waterfront, the Bund, still remain, but other well-known establishments have completely changed: the Hong Kong and Shanghai Banking Corporation, for example, now houses the city government, and the former British consulate is now a club for seamen.

Shanghai is now a great centre of light industry. It is said to possess more

(*Above*) China's course is set – to catch up with the most advanced nations of the world by the end of this century. It is a formidable task and in this poster on a Shanghai wall it is given a feverish – even apocalyptical – air by the clock in the background and the determination on the faces of the riders. The characters read: 'Take advantage of every minute and second to race to the year 2,000!' Whether China will catch up with American technology is uncertain but given sane leadership the Chinese will certainly make formidable progress.

than 9,000 factories and production centres, turning out ships, machinery, electronic equipment, meters and instruments, chemicals and textiles. Most of the machinery for China's textile mills is made here, as is a third of all China's consumer goods.

The city supplies skills as well as goods. Shanghai's technicians and workers are sent all over China to start new factories and iron out production problems, while several million citizens, including students, have gone to remote areas in the last two decades, to help develop new towns or to help peasants improve their yields. However, numbers of young people, finding conditions too tough in the harsh outlying regions, have come quietly back to Shanghai to live on the black market, creating social problems for the municipal government.

Despite all the modern development and industry, Shanghai remains a traditionally Chinese city. Square-sailed junks glide slowly along the Huang-pu (Whang-poo) River past tugs and large cargo ships; many varieties of excellent Chinese food are served in the packed restaurants; and despite big housing programmes there is still a shortage of accommodation so that many still live in the traditionally crowded conditions.

There are more public parks than in the old days; the city's famous racecourse is now one of them. And grass and bushes have been planted along one section of the waterfront Bund. This is an area favoured by young people for evening walks.

Shanghai is changing all the time. For women, the severe Mao-style uniform is giving way to skirts and gaily-patterned dresses. Hairstyles are less austere. Any move to break away from official formalities and conventions usually originates in this city or wins immediate support here. And more changes lie ahead. For if China continues her plan of inviting foreign experts to help her modernize, if foreign technology and skills flow into China on a massive scale, then Shanghai will be the first to feel the effects and reflect them.

(*Above*) Shanghai is better known for its port and factories than its temples; but the Temple of the Jade Buddha in the western section of the city has two impressive statues of the Buddha in white jade which were brought from Burma by a Chinese monk a hundred years ago. Temple roofs curve upwards so that descending demons may be directed into the air again instead of reaching the earth.

(*Right*) Before breakfast men and women all over China enjoy the gentle form of exercise known as Tai Ji Chuan (Shadow-boxing) a milder form of the more aggressive Kung Fu seen in films. Tai Ji is said to have been developed as long ago as the Sung Dynasty, (960–1126) but for centuries the knowledge of its 450 movements grouped into 36 'patterns' was confined to the nobility. Now it is officially encouraged.

(*Above*) The sign on the train says "Shanghai to Urumchi Express" – a distance of more than 2,000 miles to the Far West. The sounds of the Chinese characters are printed in romanised letters underneath in order to familiarise people with the use of latin script. The long-term aim is to use latin script for printing the Chinese language in phonetic form, but there are many obstacles, including the varying pronounciations of the common speech (Pu Tong Hua) in different provinces.

(*Left*) From a trading and business centre Shanghai has developed into an enormous industrial city where they make everything from textiles to ships to heavy machinery. Nearly all the carpets being made here are for export.

From earliest times puppet shows have been one of the most popular forms of entertainment for Chinese people – and it made little difference whether they were sophisticated Shanghai dwellers or simple villagers. High-pitched puppet voices mouth eternal truths about human nature. Travelling puppet shows have satirised emperors and tyrants by the most oblique reference. High on the repertoire for generations was "Journey to the West", otherwise known as "Monkey", which tells the story of how the all-wise monkey, possessed of Taoist wisdom, travels to the West to receive the knowledge of Buddhism, and meets with extraordinary adventures on the way, upsetting the bureaucracy of Heaven and causing hilarious upsets there. A theme like this was obviously viewed askance by Jiang Qing (Chiang Ch'ing) the wife of Chairman Mao and puppet shows generally were severely censored while she still exercised power. Now 'Monkey' has been admitted to the repertoire again. This scene shows Monkey swinging his lance and sending the heavenly host reeling in all directions.

The Water Country

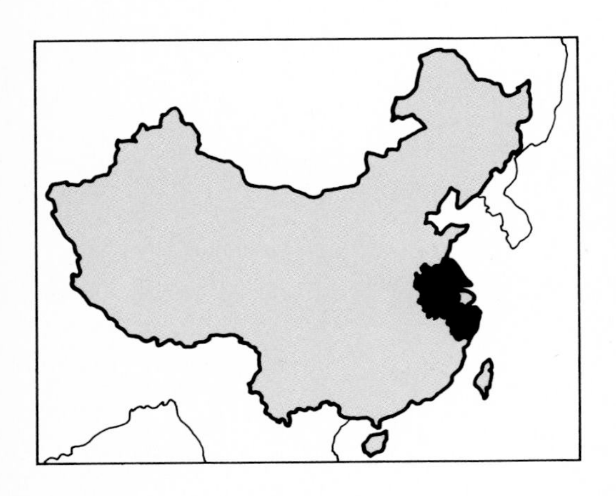

In the low-lying farmland and lake area around Shanghai small picturesque cities and beauty spots have attracted emperors and poets down the ages. Many old Chinese romances – of the teahouse girl falling in love with the penniless student, who by passing the imperial examinations wins a life of power and riches; of great families brought low; of intriguing generals and powerful concubines – have their setting in the lakeside towns of this area of east China. It is known as the 'Water Country'. Travellers are said to meet a stream every few hundred yards, and the peasants use boats as often as country people in the north use carts.

Lakes and rivers in the basin of the great Lake Tai account for 15 per cent of the total area of the Lower Yangtze region. One of the better known towns around Lake Tai is Wuxi (Wusih). The water of one of its clear springs was described by the T'ang writer Lu Yu as 'second under heaven for making tea'. Wuxi is also famous for its beautiful gardens and parks. Within the walls of the small Chichang Garden, built 470 years ago, winding, covered galleries connect pavilions round a little lake. The Plum Garden on Xushan Hill, a few miles west of the city, yields the fruit from which a Wuxi delicacy is made – honeyed plums flavoured with the essence of sweet osmanthus blossoms. Wuxi is also

(*Right*) The lakes and streams of seaside Jiangsu (Kiangsu) province support millions of ducks. And most of them are sent north to be eaten as famous Peking duck or south to become Canton duck in the restaurants of Guangzhou.

(*Far right*) Lotus-flowers in the lake, an ancient bridge, willows . . . to these calm enjoyments a disillusioned statesman would retire when the emperor's friendship turned sour. It is called the West Lake because it lies on the western side of Hangzhou city. This whole area was famous in the past for the joys of civilized living. 'So many pleasures are to be found here,' wrote the traveller Marco Polo, 'that a man fancies himself to be in paradise'.

(*Above*) Many houses in ancient Suzhou have one door opening on to the street and another on to one of the canals that criss-cross this ancient city. The Grand Canal, with its typical hump-backed bridges, was built to carry rice up to Peking for tax payment, and passes close by Suzhou.

well-known for the clay dolls and figurines made in its local workshops, and for its silk-worm cultivation that dates back 1,500 years.

Further round the lake is the city of Suzhou (Soochow), which in olden times is said to have had more beautiful girls than any other Chinese city. The reason for this may have been that when government officials scoured China for the best-looking girls for the emperor's palace, they would bring many of them to Suzhou before making their selections. Those finally chosen would be sent by boat up the Grand Canal to Peking and the runners-up would be obliged to stay on in Suzhou until they could find transport to take them back to their homes.

Suzhou is called China's Venice because of the network of canals criss-crossing the city. Its surrounding hills and lakes are also charming; the Hu Chiu Hill (Tiger Hill) is a special favourite of the local people. Suzhou also preserved ancient pagodas and the delicate Bao Dai Bridge (Precious Belt) as part of the national heritage. But it is the gardens and parks that attract most visitors to Suzhou. They are said to be the finest specimens of the art of garden design in China. Rocks from Lake Tai have been arranged among streams that flow past pavilions situated among trees and flowers.

Around Suzhou the fertile soil yields increasing harvests of rice, wheat and oil-bearing crops, and the well-known jasmine tea of Tiger Hill is much sought after. Like Wuxi, this is a celebrated area for silk-cultivation, and Suzhou

embroidery and brocades are also famous.

South of Lake Tai lies the coastal province of Zhejiang (Chekiang); which possesses one of the great beauty-spots of China – the ancient city of Hangzhou (Hangchow) with its fairytale West Lake dotted with landscaped islands reached by delicate bridges.

Hangzhou's history goes back more than 2,000 years, and the scenery of the West Lake has been famous since the time of the T'ang dynasty. One of the lake islands was built artificially in 1607. It is reached by zigzagging bridges, and its terraces and pavilions have been arranged to present delightful views. South of this island three small towers rise from the water; moonlight shining through holes in the towers and reflected from the lake has given this spot the name 'Three Pools Mirroring the Moon'. Cutting right across the lake from north to south is the Su Causeway, built during the Sung dynasty (960-1126), when the poet Su Tung-po was appointed prefect of Hangzhou. On the south bank of the lake is a park called 'Orioles Singing in the Willows', and throughout the area are hills famous for their caves, streams, rock-carvings and the Monastery of Soul's Retreat.

It was to Hangzhou that a man of refinement would come to watch the moonlight on the water, write poetry while listening with friends to the softly falling rain on the lotuses, or stroll in the gardens with their pools of brightly

(*Above*) Throughout most of central and southern China every commune has its fish ponds. After rice and wheat, fish farming is one of the most important occupations. Different breeds of fish are cultivated at different levels of the same pond. And the basin of the Yangtze – the Water Country – is where more fish are bred and eaten than anywhere else in China.

coloured fish. An ancient saying has it: 'Above is Paradise; on Earth we have Suzhou and Hangzhou.'

The ancient city of Shaoxing (Shaosing) in east Chekiang is the birthplace of China's famous modern writer, Lu Xun (Lu Hsun). He spent his boyhood there and was the friend of peasants' sons. He also knew the insides of pawnbrokers' and pharmacists' shops; his father died of a long illness and the family fell on hard days. Today visitors to the Lu Xun Memorial Hall can see his manuscripts and letters.

Shaoxing is also noted for its beautiful East Lake and its wine, first produced 2,000 years ago and now ranked among China's eight outstanding alcoholic drinks. It is made from rice and served warm, and it tastes a little like sherry. There is no better accompaniment to Chinese food.

South of Hangzhou the Qiantang (Chientang) River flows east into the sea, and every year, just after the mid-autumn festival in September, crowds throng the estuary to watch the strange phenomenon of the Qiantang River tides foaming against the sea walls. It begins as a silver line across the horizon, approaching and growing with a noise of thunder until it can be seen as a line of foaming billows more than 12 feet high. This is the Angry Tide, or East Tide. Before it can subside, another line of high waves sweeps up from the south, collides with the East Tide and sends columns of water spouting high in the air.

The waves are the result of high equinoctial tides being driven by strong winds through the funnel shape of the estuary. In August 1974 a typhoon striking south of the Qiantang River just at the time of the tides caused record high-water levels and damage to the sea-walls. However, most of the coastal crops were saved.

(*Above*) The farmer living and working in a Chinese commune must expect to spend weeks of every year digging or carting soil on some scheme of conservancy or flood prevention which will benefit other villages' production teams besides his own. In the densely populated plains of China, the two great enemies are flood and drought. A big flood control scheme has been completed around Hangzhou's West Lake.

(*Far left*) China has always been famous for the extraordinary achievements of its craftsmen – in jade and ivory carving, the most delicate embroidery and painting on silk or sandalwood. Painting fans is an old industry and in Suzhou modern newcomers may find it hard to equal the standards of the past. It used to be centred in people's own homes, now they work in organized factories.

(*Above right*) Traditionally in China a marriage without children is a catastrophe for there will be no one left to visit the family grave and revere the ancestors. Nowadays parents are urged to limit families but young children are loved and cared for as in most Asian countries. At this primary school in Wusih the wall-slogan says: 'Unite closely.'

(*Below right*) Where the land is rich (like the Hangzhou area) they harvest several crops in a year from the same fields – two yields of rice and another crop in between. Here it is green vegetables which the women are washing in the stream.

(*Far right*) The inescapable factor of China is its enormous size. Even almost a thousand million Chinese people seem dwarfed by the immensities of plain, river and lake. Chinese painting has always emphasized the dominating presence of nature, with great mountains crowned with forests and wreathed in mists, and man appearing only as a minute horseman on a remote hillside, or a boat on the great West Lake.

Yunnan and Guizhou

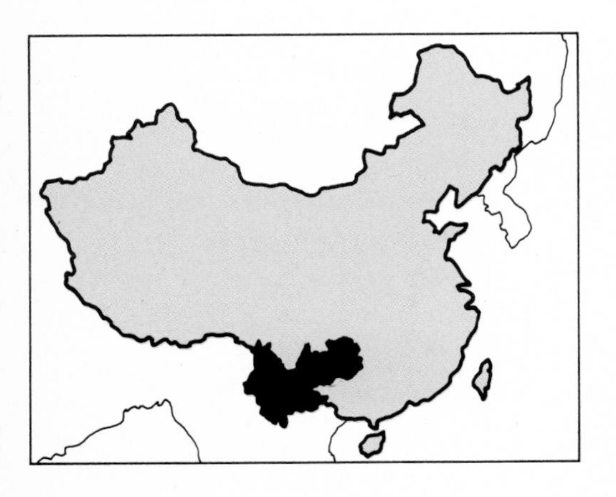

The strange and beautiful land of Yunnan ('South of the Clouds') spreads down to China's frontiers with Vietnam, Laos and Burma. It is so far from Peking, and in ancient times was so inaccessible because of its wild mountains and lack of roads, that for long periods of its history it was governed by local chieftains, running their own small highland kingdoms.

Yunnan is a land of flowers – camellias, azaleas, rhododendrons – and enormous forests. Its timber was once hauled all the way to Peking to build the columns of imperial palaces. The forests shelter elephants, pandas and parrots, and the vegetation is more varied than that of any other Chinese province. The climate ranges from icily cold to tropically hot, depending on the height above sea-level. Below 5,000 feet it is very hot and wet; above that level, up to 10,000 feet, the air is cool and refreshing.

The capital, Kunming, which stands at the northern end of an enormous lake, is called 'the City of Eternal Spring' – though some travellers say this spring is fresh enough to require warm clothing. But the sky is generally a cloudless blue, and magnolias and azaleas abound, along with tropical and sub-tropical fruits.

The human scene is brightened by the costumes and festivals of the area's many minority groups, more than 20 of which (out of a total of 50 or so spread thinly over China's western expanses) live in Yunnan, making up about a third of the province's 28 million inhabitants. There are the Yi in the northeast; the Bai and Na Xi in the northwest; the Tai in the southwest; and the Lisu, Jing Po and Wa near the Burmese frontier. Some are Buddhists, some Muslims. The groups often spread across the frontier into villages in the lands of China's neighbours.

(*Right*) Of the 22 minority peoples living in Yunnan province, the Tais are among the eight who have their own written language. Theirs is one in a closely-linked family of languages found in Thailand, Laos, Burma, N.E. India and Vietnam. Nearly all of the Tai people are Buddhists and most inhabit the lowlands as rice farmers.

(*Far right*) Great rivers rise in the Tibetan snows and flow down through Yunnan province into the lands beyond China's borders to reach the distant Pacific. In the high mountains these rivers plunge through steep narrow gorges but when they reach Yunnan's southern areas the river valleys open out, with many upland plains and fertile irrigated fields. Here the Tais, Lisus and other minority peoples make their homes. Along the valley of the Salween River winds the Burma Road where many prisoners of war died to build a communications link to supply Japan's armies.

(*Above*) Belonging to one of the minority races in China means freedom from the pressures applied to those of the main Han (Chinese) race to marry late and have only one or two children. The Yi people number about three and a half million and most of them live in Yunnan and Guizhou and the western mountains of Sichuan province.

Ancient shrines, temples and burial places in the mountains have yielded records of the period from the 3rd century BC to the 10th century AD when the chieftains of Yunnan were left more or less undisturbed by the rulers of the Han and T'ang dynasties in Peking. It was not until Genghis Khan's Mongols penetrated the mountain fastnesses in the 13th century and killed the local chieftains that the rule of Peking was enforced in Yunnan. The Venetian traveller Marco Polo visited Yunnan 700 years ago and described it as a great and noble kingdom where the people grew rich by the sale of salt, ate raw meat and followed Islam.

Until well into this century the province was still a strange, remote place, protected by its walls of rock and mountains. Even today the western half is very thinly peopled. And in the east the high plateau is broken occasionally by small plains and valleys where the highland people can live, in small tight communities of farmers. This eastern part of Yunnan has a karst landscape – limestone rocks and hills sometimes resembling forests of stone, sometimes forming overhanging, threatening cliffs, columns and spires. In this area clear streams disappear to form underground lakes and later reappear miles away. Natural limestone bridges span many of the rivers.

Western Yunnan is very different. High mountain ranges run north and south, separated by narrow valleys that carry the upper streams of rivers such as the Lan Cang (Mekong) and the Nu Jiang (Salween). Where the river valleys are narrowest, two people standing on the high summits of opposite banks can nearly hear each other if they shout across, but if one of them wishes to meet the other it will take him a whole day to climb down one hill and up the other. The currents of these rivers are too fast for navigation, but they can sometimes be spanned by overhanging rope bridges. Earthquakes are frequent in this area, because the earth's crust here was formed in a later geological age than the crust elsewhere.

In former days Yunnan was notorious for opium growing and trafficking. About one fifth of the province's farmland was given over to the opium poppy, and war lords became millionaires from the sale of its extract. In old China opium was known as 'Yunnan earth', and Kunming, the capital of the province, was the centre of China's opium trade. The city had more than 2,000 opium dens and 12 per cent of the people were addicts. When the Americans used Yunnan as a military base in World War Two, the cultivation of the poppy was considerably reduced. Now it is banned entirely, and it is claimed that no trace of the old addiction remains – although opium poppies are still grown across the border in Laos and Burma.

(*Above*) A high plateau reaches over the eastern part of Yunnan and covers the whole of the neighbouring province of Guizhou. Scattered throughout the plateau are small valleys where it is possible to terrace the land and grow rice. This is still a remote and relatively backward part of China, but the Chinese report great progress in wiping out disease and providing schools.

One of the biggest changes to affect Yunnan has been the development of road, rail and air links with the outside world. The railway linking Kunming with the main cities of adjoining Sichuan province is one of the great engineering feats of modern times. The journey by rail from Kunming to Chengtu, in Sichuan, takes 24 hours. The 680 miles of track connecting the two cities passes through 427 tunnels (one of them nearly 4 miles long) and over 653 bridges.

The eastern plateau region of Yunnan spreads to the neighbouring province of Guizhou (Kweichow). It used to be said that this area was so poor that when a family wished to eat fish, the father would hang a paper cut-out of a fish on the wall. The family would watch it while they ate their miserable portion of rice and simulated belching to give themselves the illusion they were eating well. It was also said of this province that there was not a level metre of land to be found in it, nor an ounce of silver, nor a pound of rice.

Although it is true that the topsoil of Guizhou is very thin and stony and that harvests can be increased only by terracing fresh land out of unpromising hill-slopes, the tobacco grown here is famous throughout China, and so is the spirit distilled at the town of Mao Tai. This liquor – colourless and with somewhat more body than vodka – is not only drunk at every Chinese banquet and celebration but is now exported to the United States and Europe. In addition to tobacco and liquor the province also yields gold, silver, copper and mercury.

Guizhou's history is unusual. As in neighbouring Yunnan, minority groups abound, and for centuries Guizhou was ruled by chieftains of the Miao people, who lived in walled towns and enjoyed almost total independence apart from their annual payment of tribute to the emperor. But in the 18th century imperial officials greedy for power and Chinese farmers seeking land turned their gaze towards the province. And after prolonged and bitter fighting, Guizhou finally came under Peking's yoke.

The capital of the province, Guiyang (Kweiyang), is an important road and rail centre. Further north lies the city of Tsunyi, famous in the annals of the Chinese Communist Party because it was here, during the Long March in the mid-1930s, that the party meeting was held at which Mao Tse-tung assumed the leadership of the party, a leadership he was to hold for the rest of his life – with far-reaching effects on the lives of all Chinese.

(Right) Mountain ranges in Yunnan have been the result of violent folding. Where faults occur in the earth's crust they have sometimes filled with water to form vast lakes. According to legend Kunming, the capital of Yunnan, was once part of an ancient sea that covered Yunnan and Guizhou provinces. After violent natural upheavals this sea disappeared leaving only the beautiful Dian Chi Lake at the foot of the cliff-like Western Hill.

(Right) The Er Hai Lake, with the town of Dali on its western shore is another lake created by earlier movement of the earth's crust and famous for its beautiful scenery. The lake is a few miles across but 25 miles from north to south. Eighteen rivers flow into it, and in the neighbourhood is quarried some of the world's most beautiful marble.

Canton and The South-East

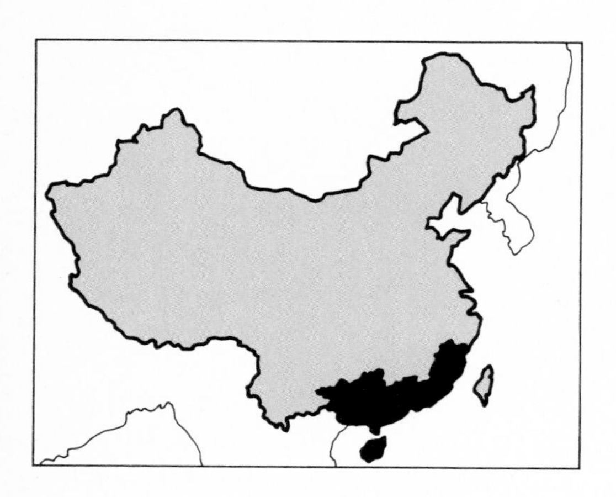

The southeast coastal provinces of China are the homeland of nearly all those Chinese who have gone abroad to seek their fortunes. As many as 20 million Chinese are now living and working in 'the Southern Ocean' (the Chinese name for Southeast Asia) and in more distant lands – Australia, Britain, the United States and Canada.

These overseas Chinese have often maintained contact with families left behind, sending home money to support relatives and sometimes in old age returning to their native villages to die. But many have become citizens of the countries where they settled, and their children and grandchildren have grown up there. In Southeast Asia the overseas Chinese sometimes remain poor farmers, but more often they are the shopkeepers and traders, shrewd operators in the markets; some have even become millionaires. In some cases an overseas Chinese community has incurred the wrath of the local people because it hoards grain in hard times or influences the government through corruption.

Most of the emigrants have come from two provinces on the southeast coast – Guangdong (Kwangtung) and Fujian (Fukien) – many of them going to work as contract labour on the plantations of Borneo or in the Malayan tin mines.

In earlier centuries the Chinese were already visiting other countries for trade, exporting porcelain and silks in return for resins, rhinoceros horn, gold and other metals. Long ago the great city of Canton established relations with foreign traders and became the largest seaport in south China and the gateway to the country. Arab traders travelled to it across the Indian ocean, and a mosque was built in the city as early as the 7th century. Now the population numbers more than 2 million, and Canton is still growing. It engages in light industry, silk weaving, pottery and food-processing.

(*Right*) Canton is in the tropics and the summers are wet and very hot. So the Pearl river is the obvious place for relaxation, and this was true even before Chairman Mao made his famous swim across the Yangtze.

(*Far right*) Canton's Pearl River Square is a huge open space bordering on the river and across it can be seen the buildings of the exhibition halls where exhibits of the Canton Trade Fair are on show. Canton has more than two million people and most of them seem to be in the streets at any one time, especially when some festival or propaganda show is underway.

战无不胜的毛泽东思想万

(*Above*) In the big southern province of Guangdong farm life varies greatly from one commune to another. In some areas they grow mainly rice, elsewhere all the effort is in mulberry trees (for silkworms) and fishponds. Near a big city much of the land will be given up to vegetable farming – thousands of tons of vegetables are shipped into Canton every day from the surrounding countryside. And many communes near cities will earn extra income by doing sub-contract work – making minor components for the big factories in town.

Like Shanghai, Canton has always been more aware than the rest of China of the outside world and long ago had to cope with the pressures of Western merchants greedy for supplies of Chinese silk and tea and for fortunes to be made from smuggling opium into China from India. In 1839 the Chinese Commissioner in Canton ordered British opium cargoes to be destroyed, and after the Opium War with Britain which followed, China was obliged to cede Hong Kong to the British. The Portuguese had already possessed the nearby promontory of Macau (Macao) since 1557. Today Hong Kong, which remains a British territory, is a thriving industrial port and city of 4¾ million people, nearly all of them Chinese. There is a small community of British administrators and businessmen and a military garrison. Both Hong Kong and Macau are on excellent terms with the present Chinese government and have been given the green light to develop and expand.

Twice a year in Canton, in huge exhibition halls near the Pearl River, the authorities hold an Export Trade Fair which attracts thousands of businessmen from all over the world. Canton's main hotel, the Dong Fang, is packed to bursting; entertainments and excursions are organized for the visitors. Apart from businessmen, increasing numbers of tourists are visiting Canton, and from there going on by plane or train to other parts of China.

Cantonese food is famous throughout China, and the Cantonese are as interested in cuisine as the French. The food is of great delicacy, and the ingredients are cooked rapidly to maintain their full flavour. Unique to Cantonese restaurants are *Dim Sun* (small hearts), little stuffed dumplings and other titbits carried round the tables on trays or trolleys. In winter, snakes are served – treated in various ways to provide a soup and other courses.

This southeast coastal region is subject to typhoons – huge circular storms with wind speeds sometimes rising to nearly 100 miles an hour. They form over the Pacific and move towards the Chinese coast like aerial whirlpools. In the days before early warning systems, the loss of life and damage to buildings and crops was horrifying. Now signal stations and improved meteorological reporting do much to save property, and a hardy form of short-stalked rice has been

developed to withstand the onslaught of typhoon rain and wind.

The high rainfall and tropical heat prevalent for much of the year are very good for rice- and fruit-farming. Parts of Guangdong province produce two and even three annual crops of rice and something like 300 kinds of fruit, including lychees. These have rough husks and a hard nut, but the pale juicy flesh is delicious. A branch of a particularly prized tree loaded with fruit will fetch high prices at a Hong Kong auction. Legend tells of a Chinese emperor in Peking who sent a special mission all the way down to Canton, travelling post-haste day and night, to make sure of the pick of the crop for a beloved concubine.

Some villages in Guangdong grow scarcely any rice but spend all their time and effort on silk-worm cultivation. The worms feed on mulberry leaves before making their cocoons, which are then gathered and unravelled into the finest thread. In this part of the world seven or eight harvests a year can be gathered.

Fu Jian, the next province up the coast from Guangdong, is nearly all mountain apart from the lower reaches of its rivers and the coastal strip. The story of Fu Jian is the story of its ports – Fu Zhou (Foochow), Amoy and Quanzhou (Chuanchow). They have been busy trading centres for hundreds of years, and in pre-communist days a steady stream of emigrants passed through them to start a new life overseas.

Westwards from Guangdong is Guangxi province, officially known as the Guangxi Zhuang (Kwangsi Chuang) Autonomous Region. The Zhuang are the biggest minority group in China, and most of them live in Guangxi. Like parts of the far southwest, the hills of Guangxi are largely limestone, and some areas form a forest of limestone pinnacles and spires, with winding caverns and underground lakes below. This landscape is at its most impressive near the large town of Guilin (Kweilin). Even northerners agree with the saying that Guilin is 'unparalleled throughout the whole world'. South of Guangdong province is the large tropical island of Hainan, which produces sugar, rubber and tropical fruits. Its plains are hot and wet, but the hills provide cool relief at night.

(*Above*) Planting out the rice seedlings is a back-breaking job for the farmer. If the land is fertile enough it may need doing two or even three times a year. Mechanical rice-planters have been tried and these are practicable where there are large level fields, but not in uneven soil or where there is terracing. The danger to the farmer comes from schistosomiasis – a snail-borne disease – when he works in water for long periods. Progress has been claimed in combating the disease but it has not yet been brought completely under control.

View of the bustling capitalist colony of Hong Kong seen from the Peak, the highest hill on Hong Kong island. Most of Hong Kong's 404 square miles are steep hills and islands and most of the colony's 4.7 million are packed into the area on either side of the harbour shown here. Expensive residential blocks are in the foreground with banks and offices nearer the waterfront. Across the busy harbour lies Kowloon, with the landing-strip of Hong Kong Airport showing as a thin slip of land running out into the bay below the distant hills. And beyond the hills lie the New Territories which stretch right up to the Chinese border twenty miles away and make up four-fifths of Hong Kong's total area. They were obtained from China under a lease due to expire in 1997, but the Chinese Government has encouraged Hong Kong to prosper because this also benefits China. Hundreds of immigrants from China arrive daily.

(*Above*) Year by year China realises the enormous potential of its lakes and rivers to provide the energy needed for the Four Modernizations Programme. China is rich in energy resources – there are abundant supplies of coal and oil still to be exploited. The only problems now are in sinking new mines, drilling in the off-shore oil areas, and harnessing the swift-running rivers. The Qing Shi Tang (Green Lion Plant) hydro-electric station supplies the Guilin area in Guangxi province.

(*Right*) The vast plains of the Pearl River Delta are criss-crossed by streams and irrigation ditches that also serve as communication links.

(*Far right*) A continuous job for the villagers is to keep the irrigation ditches clear – even in the rain. This ancient type of raincape make from overlapping straw is very effective though plastic is steadily taking over.

(*Above*) Shamian Island with its Anglican church is at the south-west tip of Canton like a boat moored alongside the city. Shamian Island used to be the area of French and British concessions – land made available to the two governments when the Chinese allowed trade to develop after the Opium Wars. The island became an exclusively European area and no Chinese were allowed there without permission. There were tennis courts, a yacht club and pleasant houses. The spacious homes are now used for schools and government offices. The church is now used as a meeting hall.

(*Right*) A pagoda not far from Canton. In China pagodas are watch-towers, pleasure-houses, commemorative acts of piety, towers of remembrance – and a style of architecture unknown elsewhere in the world.

(*Far right*) The conical straw hat to keep off the sun and rain, and the shoulder-pole for carrying heavy burdens – these are the symbols of life in the countryside since time immemorial, and even today the shoulder-pole is the only way to transport goods where roads are few and footpaths narrow.

Index

Numbers in italics refer to illustrations and captions

Acknowledgements

The publishers would like to thank the following organizations and individuals for their kind permission to reproduce the photographs in this book.

Aspect Picture Library 76, (Alex Langley) 7, 60, 78 below, 93, 95; Colorific, (Charlotte Bourdier) 90–91; Explorer, (C. Cros) 61 above; Richard and Sally Greenhill, 8, 74, 77; Susan Griggs Agency, (Peter Griffiths) 22 above and below, 35 below; Sonia Halliday, (Jane Taylor) 2–3, 28, 30–31, 92 above; Robert Harding Associates, 9, 18, 19 below, 25, 92 below, (Nigel Cameron) 81, 83, 84–85 above and below, (P. S. Ibbotson) 40, 72, (Tim Megarry) 26 above left, 45, 62 below; John Hillelson Agency 15, (James Andanson/Sygma) 38 inset, (Bruno Barbey/Magnum) 39 inset, 55, 62 above, 78 above, 94 right, (Brian Brake) 80, (Rene Burri/Magnum) 19 above, 35 above, 48, (Henri Cartier-Bresson/ Magnum) 17, (Dr. Georg Gerster) 20, (Felix Greene) 50, 51, 53, (Marc Riboud/Magnum) 11, 14, 27 above left and right, 82, (Han Suyin/Magnum) 52 above and below; Alan Hutchison, 69 below; Paolo Koch, 21, 26 above right and below, 31 inset, 32 below, 36 above and below, 41, 42, 43 above and below, 44, 46–47, 54, 61 below, 64, 66, 67, 68 above, 69 above, 70–71, 94 above left; Christian Leprette, Endpapers (front), 38–39; Leung Kui Ting, 1; William MacQuitty, 63; Raymond Pask, 58–59, 73, 75, 79, 89; Van Phillips, 12–13, 29, 32 above, 33, 34, 88; Rapho, (Berhaut) 23, (Jerry Cooke) 86, (Landau) 49, 56, 57, (G. Silberstein) 68 below; Top Agence, (E. Boubat) 10; Zefa, (J. Bitsch) 37, (Hermann Engel) 65, (Dr. H. Kramarz) 87.

40
45
50